Railway Masterpieces

Brian Solomon

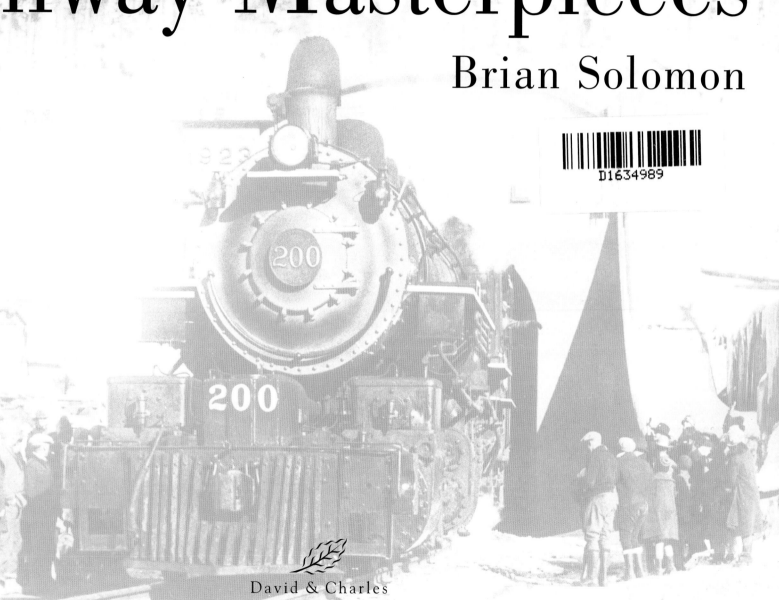

David & Charles

ABOUT THE AUTHOR

Brian Solomon grew up in Monson, Massachusetts. He divides his time between Ireland and America while writing about photographing railway operations in Europe, America and Japan. He has a BFA in Photographic Illustration from the Rochester Institute of Technology, New York. He is a past editor of Pacific RailNews, and has contributed to many railway publications including TRAINS Magazine, Railway Age, CTC Board, and the Irish Record Society Journal.

A DAVID & CHARLES BOOK

First published in the UK in 2003
First published in the USA in 2002 by Krause Publications, Iola

A catalogue record for this book is available from the British Library.

ISBN 0 7153 1743 1 paperback

Printed in China by Sun Fung Offset Binding Co., Ltd.
for David & Charles
Brunel House   Newton Abbot   Devon

All photos by Brian Solomon unless otherwise noted.

Cover Photo:
Under and over at Starrucca Viaduct on May 13, 1972; Erie-Lackawanna NE-74 is eastbound on the bridge, while D&H RW-6 rests beneath the bridge. Photo by Jim Shaughnessy.

Visit our website at www.davidandcharles.co.uk

David & Charles books are available from all good bookshops; alternatively you can contact our Orderline on (0)1626 334555 or write to us at FREEPOST EX2 110, David & Charles Direct, Newton Abbot, TQ12 4ZZ (no stamp required UK mainland).

Printed in China.

Dedication

To my Mother

Acknowledgments

A book spanning considerable time and geography could not have been completed without help from many people. I am grateful to everyone who participated and helped me along the way. Since my railway interests are not focused on a singular topic, nor on a sole project, it is difficult to assess where the work on the book began and, even with the completion of this volume, my interest in the topics discussed will not cease. I'm always searching for new information, new perspectives, and new images of railways in the United States, Europe, and everywhere around the world.

Thanks to Don Gulbrandsen of Krause Publishing who enthusiastically embraced the concept for this book when I first mentioned it to him several years ago. Don and I have worked together for nearly a decade on various railway publications, including *Pacific RailNews* which he hired me to help edit in 1994. Thanks to the editorial and production staff at Krause, including Christine Townsend and Marilyn Hochstatter, for their efforts. Special thanks are due my father, Richard Jay Solomon, from whom I inherited my railway passion, and who has generously lent me the use of his extensive and ever-growing library, as well as his photographs for use in this text. He suggested inclusion of many of the topics in this book, as well as those that I ultimately chose to save for a future volume. In addition he proofread much of the text.

Several people were especially helpful in tracking down information. John Gruber helped compose sections on the Kate Shelley Bridge and Tulip Trestle, and was generous with information and his photography. Markku Pulkkinen assisted me with the Helsinki Station, Finnish and German translation work, and tracking down details on the Swedish Rc and German Class 103. Alistair Mearns of Edinburgh helped find information on the Firth of Forth Bridge, and with the proofreading of topics in Great Britain. Alan Reekie has been very helpful over the years, especially with information on high-speed railways and operations in continental Europe. William S. Young graciously provided John Gruber and me with a tour of Susquehanna, Pennsylvania and its environs, and he is responsible for much original research on the Starrucca and Tunkhannock Viaducts. Brian Jennison and J.D Schmid inspired my interest in the Southern Pacific and helped put its great Tehachapi crossing in perspective. Tom Kline tracked down information on the Cascade Tunnel. Robert A. Buck of Tucker's Hobbies (Warren, Massachusetts) has helped in so many ways it would impossible to list them all, but his lifelong interest in the Boston & Albany inspired my own fascination with the railroad and its history. Thanks to Paul Carver and George C. Corey for discussion and information on steam locomotives and matters relating to the New York Central. My friend Tom Hoover has helped me better understand how diesel locomotives work, and accompanied me on many trips to photograph railways as well as a daring Hoosac Tunnel adventure many years ago. The folks at the Irish Railway Record Society in Dublin have provided me the use of their library and lent expertise, which has helped not just in the understanding of Irish railways, but in railway operations around the world. Thanks to Robert W. Jones for his common interest in the Boston & Albany, and to Doug Riddell for providing a tour of Washington Union Station and inspiration through his own writings.

Photography has played a very important role in my interest in railways as well as in the illustration of this book. In addition to my photographs and those of my father's, many others have provided work for consideration in this book. Tom Kline, Jim Shaughnessy, Tim Doherty, Brian Jennison, Mike Gardner, William D. Middleton, Eric Hendrickson, Doug Eisele, Mel Patrick, George C. Corey, and Robert A. Buck all provided images. Also thanks to John P. Hankey, Dennis Lebeau, Milepost 92-1/2, Jay Williams, Bob's Photo, J.R Quinn, and the Denver Public Library for lending me photos from their collections. Special thanks to Fred Matthews, who has managed to capture the grandeur of St. Pancras train shed more effectively than anyone else I know. Photographic support is also important; thanks to Mike Gardner, and the Gallery of Photography (Dublin) for the use of their black-and-white darkroom facilities, Photo Care on Abbey Street (Dublin), and to E.B Luce (Worcester, Massachusetts) for E-6 processing, and to everyone at John Gunn's Camera (Dublin) for photographic supplies and aesthetic criticism. Thanks to Diarmaid Collins for his map graphics, and to Doug Moore for help with copy work.

Many people have hosted me on my travels and accompanied me on photographic expeditions. Thanks to Dave and Helen Burton for visits to Tehachapi; my brother Seán for trips to Philadelphia, Delaware, and Chicago (among other venues); Mel Patrick for visits to Colorado; Tessa Bold for visits to Oxford, London, and Bonn, as well as entertaining me with her humor, and political and economic perspectives; Asoa Ishizuka for help in Japan; the Hoover family for numerous visits to Pennsylvania; George Pitarys for trips around New England and eastern Canada; to Claire Nolan of Alki Tours for giving me the opportunity to ride through the Cascade Tunnel; David Hegerty for visits in London and trips to England, Wales, and Ireland; and to my college roommate Bob for visits in Washington, D.C. and Pittsburgh as well photographic support over the years; John P. Hankey for detailed tours of the Baltimore & Ohio and intellectual discussion of B&O history. My mother, Maureen Solomon, has been especially tolerant of our family's keen railway interest over the years (and the mountains of books and photos that clutter the house), and has helped with bookkeeping and other details during my prolonged travels.

Brian Solomon, Dublin 2002

Table of Contents

The Tunkhannock Viaduct looms large over the village of Nicholson, Pennsylvania.

Introduction

The bright spring sun shines on Conrail TV301, a westbound double stack, as it rolls westward across Starrucca Viaduct in May 1989. The old Erie Railroad was well suited to double stack trains, which have a taller profile than traditional freight trains.

This book is a collection of images and words that portray some of the world's finest railway achievements. I have designed it as a gallery of excellence. The works displayed were selected using a variety of different criteria. Some were selected because of technical excellence, others for their aesthetic perfection, visionary execution, or exceptional marketing success. Each is impressive in its own way.

When visiting a gallery, you go to see what is displayed, not to critique flaws in the collection. A visitor to the Louvre may be awed by da Vinci's Mona Lisa—perhaps the most famous of all paintings—and inspired by a multitude of lesser-known works, but should not become incensed upon learning that Whistler's Mother (properly titled *Arrangement in Grey and Black No. 1*) is not in the Louvre's extensive collection. As it happens, Whistler's Mother is displayed in the Musée d'Orsay on the other side of the Seine, certainly a more apropos venue. Every gallery is limited by space and, likewise, this book has a finite number of pages. I've given some works more space than others. Many are well known, well documented, and familiar; others are lesser known, and a few are even obscure. I've not attempted to include all the greatest railway masterpieces, or even provide a uniform or equitable cross section of the very finest. There are any number of excellent railway stations, trains, locomotives, and engineering works that could have been included but are not. By leaving them aside, there is space for more lengthy treatment of the subjects selected. This is not a catalog, but a showcase. (Besides, this leaves material for a second volume.)

The selection of topics encompasses items from the earliest days of the railway right up to the present; from Stephenson's *Rocket* to the latest in high-speed rail technology. I have tried to put each topic in context to give the subject, as a whole, greater meaning. Often topics have a common underlying thread that ties several concepts together. There has always been an international connection in railway technology. In the early days of steam railways in Britain, engineers came from many countries to learn about the latest developments. It is no coincidence that the builders of the first American lines adopted British practices, nor is it any wonder that most knew each other fairly well. Railway technology has often crossed from one country to another. Germany's *Flying Hamburger* trains were a precursor to technological development and improved rail services around the world. The Japanese Shinkansen was derived from American technology, while the TALGO has a unique international relationship with Spain, America, and Germany.

I have put extra effort in selecting the photographs used as illustrations in this book. I am a photographer and have spent many years photographing railways around the world. Some of the images that are featured were made specifically to illustrate this project, while others were drawn from my general collection. In addition to my own photographs, I have had the privilege to draw from my father's collection, and I have also asked other photographers to lend their work to this project.

Some subjects are easier to capture than others. I made just one trip to the Leipzig Hauptbahnhof and in the course of two days' photographing, I felt I had a good body of material representing the station. By contrast, I have visited the Starrucca Viaduct a half-dozen times over the last 15 years and I'll keep going back to it again and again.

I regularly work in both color and black and white, and I'm often asked about my techniques and equipment. Presently, I do my color photography using Nikon cameras and Fuji transparency films. I use several different bodies including an F3T and an N90s, and I employ a range of lenses from 24mm to 400mm. I occasionally also use a Contax G2 range finder which has wonderfully sharp Zeiss lenses. Prior to 1997, I often used Kodachrome 25 film, which produced exceptionally sharp images. For my black-and-white photography I use an old Rolleiflex Model T with a Zeiss Tessar lens. This camera em-

ploys a square format, which lends itself well to railroad images. In addition, my Nikons are often loaded with Kodak Tri-X or Ilford HP5. From time to time, I've borrowed a range of different cameras and I've found that every type of equipment has its strengths and its weaknesses. I do my own black-and-white processing and develop my film to custom tailored chemical formulas that I've perfected over the years.

I feel it is important not to just include a photograph, but to include the right photograph. I poured over thousands of slides, prints, and negatives in order to select what I felt were the most appropriate photos for this book. Yet, as I am writing this, I have not yet seen the book that you see before you, so I can only imagine what the final product looks like, and it is my greatest hope that you are pleased with it.

Starrucca Viaduct is one of the most impressive bridges dating from the formative days of railroad building. On October 21, 2001, the morning sun illuminated the stone arches that span the valley of Starrucca Creek at Lanesboro, Pennsylvania.

Section One

LOCOMOTIVES & TRAINS

H. Bentley Crouch

The 4-4-0 American type survive in out-of-the-way places decades after they had been banished from heavy mainline services. On November 27, 1956, Canadian Pacific 4-4-0 No. 136 leads train No. 159 with a mixed consist north of Norton, New Brunswick.

Stephenson's *Rocket*

This replica of Robert Stephenson's *Rocket* at the National Railway Museum in York depicts the way it is believed to have appeared during the famous Rainhill Trials. It features a tall stack, steeply inclined cylinders, and brightly painted boiler jacketing. On this model, portions of the locomotive's cylinders and firetube boiler have been cut away for display purposes.

The railway locomotive came about as a result of the inventive efforts of many people over the course of more than a century. Crude stationary steam engines were built to power pumps in Britain beginning in the early 1700s. These were enormous, ponderous machines that used relatively low-pressure steam to act on a single cylinder. A Scot, James Watt, improved the efficiency of steam engine design through his careful studies of thermal dynamics. Among his contributions were the development of a double-acting reciprocating engine and the conversion of reciprocating motion to rotary-motion: two of the key elements needed for a self-propelled steam engine—in other words, a locomotive.

Although Watt was capable of developing a locomotive, he was morally opposed to the concept, so that its invention was left to others. In 1803, Cornishman Richard Trevithick built the first steam locomotive, known as the Pen-y-Darren engine. At this time, there were numerous guided tramways operating in quarries, collieries, and mines around Britain. These lines were precursors to the railways, using animal power to haul short trains of industrial wagons on lightly built tracks. Trevithick and others demonstrated the advantages of using a locomotive on these industrial tramways, and within two decades there were dozens of crude locomotives working on tramlines in Britain.

One of the most successful early locomotive designers was George Stephenson. In 1821, he was hired to build the Stockton & Darlington, one of Britain's first public railways. He convinced the proprietors of this line to use steam power, and in 1825 the Stockton

& Darlington became the world's first public steam-operated railway. While it used a mix of steam and animal power to haul trains in its early years, the railway attracted attention from engineers around Britain, Europe, and America who came in droves to study it. Stephenson went on to tackle an even more ambitious railway project: the construction of the Liverpool & Manchester Railway. This line was far more complicated than anything that had preceded it, and was one of the largest civil engineering projects ever undertaken up to that time. Unlike the Stockton & Darlington and early industrial tramways, the L&M was designed to connect two large cities. It was intended to carry a large volume of passengers and general freight traffic, not simply a vehicle for the movement of heavy commodities such as the coal tramways. Where the S&D relied on animal power to haul a portion of its traffic, the L&M was designed to use steam power exclusively.

By the late 1820s, the steam locomotive had made its mark, and some fifty locomotives were operating in Britain. Yet, early locomotives were clumsy, inefficient, and slow-moving contraptions prone to frequent failures. Better machines were needed if the L&M was going to solely rely upon steam for its day-to-day operations. So, prior to the completion of its line, the Liverpool & Manchester staged a widely publicized locomotive contest to encourage locomotive development. Known as the Rainhill Trials, this contest was conducted in October 1829, near the Rainhill Bridge roughly midway along the L&M route between its namesake cities. Locomotive builders were urged to enter, as long as their machines met certain prerequisites; among them were strict weight limitations and high expectations of fuel efficiency. The weight limit alone precluded many existing locomotives from participating. As the story goes, the builders of the winning locomotive would be awarded the princely sum, for those days, of £500.

Four locomotives were entered, although only three participated in the actual trials. Of the three, the machine named *Rocket*, built by George Stephenson's son Robert, was by far the most able performer. It weighed about 9,560 pounds, which conformed to the contest's weight limit, and featured a boiler six feet long, three feet by four inches in diameter, which powered a pair of 8x16.5-inch (bore and stroke) cylinders. The boiler pressure was set at approximately 50 psi, which was then considered a high-pressure engine, although typical of early locomotives. Only the *Rocket*'s front two wheels were powered, and these measured 4 feet 8.5 inches in diameter. (Interestingly, this was the same measurement used for the track gauge.) Like many early locomotives, *Rocket* featured a disproportionately tall stack that was braced by rods extending from the boiler.

During the trials, Stephenson's *Rocket* reached a top speed of 29 mph, and demonstrated reliable operation. What makes the *Rocket* significant to us today is not just its public success at the Rainhill Trials, but the combination of design features that made it vastly superior to all previous locomotive designs. The *Rocket* was a developmental milestone. Robert Stephenson had melded three principle design elements that subsequently influenced nearly all successful steam locomotives. It used a multi-tubular, firetube boiler; employed forced draft from cylinder exhaust; and featured a direct connection between the cylinders and driving wheels. While none of these features were unique to the *Rocket*, it was the first machine to combine them.

Although it set a major design precedent, the *Rocket*'s fundamental layout is significantly different from later locomotives. Its drive wheels are located ahead of the cylinders, instead of behind them. And the driving wheels are at the front of the boiler, instead of either centered below it or set toward the rear. Also, in its original configuration, *Rocket*'s cylinders were placed at a very steep angle (this was later corrected). Later locomotives featured a lower cylinder angle, and eventually many locomotives were designed with level cylinders.

Robert Stephenson benefited greatly from his ingenuity. He refined his designs and built many locomotives for railways in Britain and many other countries. His *Rocket* was recognized for its significance and preserved. The original machine, along with a replica dressed to resemble the *Rocket* as it appeared at the Rainhill Trials, are both displayed at the National Railway Museum in York. The success of the *Rocket* provided the Liverpool & Manchester with the tool it needed for successful steam operation. The railway opened in September 1830 and is considered the prototype steam railway that was emulated again and again around the world.

The original *Rocket* is also displayed at the National Railway Museum at York. While this machine is the granddaddy of successful steam locomotive design, and nearly all subsequent steam locomotive designs can be traced to the success of the *Rocket*, this machine is significantly different than most later locomotives. The *Rocket* that is presently displayed has been altered since its day in the sun at Rainhill more than 170 years ago.

Grasshopper

Vertical boiler locomotives were an anomaly to conventional locomotive practice, but they provided the Baltimore & Ohio a practical, motive-power solution in its formative years. Although the Grasshopper type was unusual, it found a niche in B&O operations and survived for nearly 60 years in regular service. This one is currently displayed at the Chicago Railroad Fair with replica passenger cars.

Otto Perry, Denver Public Library, Western History Department photo op2611

The British-born steam railway quickly caught the attention of American businessmen and engineers in the early 1800s, who saw its value as practical transportation. It is amazing how quickly the steam railway concept traveled across the ocean and took root in America, especially considering the great difficulties of intercontinental travel at the time. But perhaps more importantly, consider how different the economies were between America and Britain at the time. By 1820, Britain had had an industrial base in place for more than a century, while America was primarily an agricultural nation. In Britain, collieries, iron mines, foundries, textile mills, and other industrial concerns were common and abundant. Furthermore, a complex and extensive canal network laced the country, providing adequate, if slow, transportation for industry. By contrast, America had very little industry and minimal infrastructure. The famous Erie Canal opened in 1825, but was an exception in America's largely undeveloped transport network. Yet, there had been interest in steam-powered transport in America since the end of the 18th century. The steamboat had found its place in American transport, and cross-country railways had been suggested a full decade before the completion of the Stockton & Darlington in 1825.

In 1827, citizens of the Eastern Seaboard port of Baltimore were eyeing the western frontier—what we now call western Maryland, West Virginia, and Ohio—and chartered one of America's earliest railways, the Baltimore & Ohio. This line was designed to connect Baltimore with the Ohio River, which would provide water access to the interior of the country, thus giving Baltimore its share of traffic to the West. Baltimore hoped to benefit from the railway in the same way that New York City had profited from the Erie Canal. There were no steam railways in the United States, and the B&O dispatched a team of young engineers to Britain to learn how railways worked so as to bring the knowledge and technology back with them. George Washington Whistler (see pages 97 to 99), William Gibbs McNeil, and Jonathan Knight were among those who studied early British railway practice. Not only did they come back and help in the building of the B&O, but they became some of the foremost American railway engineers of their day. The transfer of knowledge across the ocean is evident in the large stone bridges near Baltimore, which bear a distinct similarity to early railway viaducts in Britain.

Despite its early connections with British engineering practice, the B&O soon started down a diverging path in locomotive technology. The conditions facing the B&O were different than its British counterparts. The American railroad faced rougher terrain, and had to work with less capital. As a result, the B&O was constructed with tighter curves and much more severe gradients than would be expected of British lines, and these gave the B&O different motive power needs. Although the railroad was initially operated with horses, from an early date steam power was a serious consideration.

A replica of Peter Cooper's 1830 locomotive is seen at Ellicott City, Maryland. This machine is significantly larger than the original that Peter Cooper used to demonstrate to the Baltimore & Ohio.

In 1829, the B&O ordered a Stephenson locomotive, but on its way to America the ship carrying this unfortunate machine sunk in the Irish Sea. Even had the locomotive arrived, it may have suffered the same fate as other early British imports on American lines. Delaware & Hudson, Mohawk & Hudson, and Camden & Amboy all imported British locomotives, but found their rigid wheel base ill suited to the track structure. These locomotives derailed too frequently and required substantial modification in order to be of use.

The B&O chose a homegrown solution to its motive power problem. Baltimore & Ohio historian, John P. Hankey, explains: "In 1830, New York executive Peter Cooper, who had financial interests in Baltimore, contracted for the construction of a small, one-ton steam locomotive. He intended to demonstrate that practical locomotives could be built for the B&O in America. Cooper's locomotive was largely derived from domestic marine engines and had little in common with British designs. It employed a vertical boiler and vertical cylinders. Today, Cooper's diminutive machine is often referred to in stories as the "Tom Thumb," although it was not known by that name at the time. The tiny engine convinced the B&O, which hired Cooper to build a small fleet of engines for the line. He failed at this task, and the B&O was faced with finding another locomotive supplier."

Inspired by the Liverpool & Manchester's famous Rainhill Trials in Britain, the B&O held its own locomotive competition in 1831, just a year-and-a-half later. There is some irony here: The B&O mimicked the event, rather than the machine that became the event's outcome. So where the Rainhill Trials produced the most influential locomotive design of all time—Robert Stephenson's winning *Rocket*, the locomotive from which most subsequent steam locomotives were derived—the B&O's trial fell short on practical technology. B&O's winning locomotive was a 3.5-ton machine built by Phineas Davis, named York, after the Pennsylvania city where it was constructed. This small vertical boiler machine fulfilled the spirit of B&O's specifications, but suffered from several serious mechanical flaws that made it impractical for regular service. In addition to a poor boiler design, it was too light, and had inadequate running gear.

Still, B&O was convinced that it was on the right track and hired Davis to build another locomotive for them. In 1832, he built the Atlantic, which melded successful design elements of Cooper's locomotive with those of the York. Like the other locomotives, Atlantic used a vertical boiler, but of substantially larger dimensions. This boiler, like that used by Cooper's engine and other successful designs including Stephenson's *Rocket*, was of the multitubular fire tube variety. It was 51 inches in diameter, and the stack, 13 inches in diameter, was 14 feet, 6 inches above track level. The locomotive weighed 6.5 tons. It had a pair of 10x20 inch (bore and stroke) cylinders, positioned vertically, as in the case of many early engines. Power was transmitted from the cylinders through a complex network of rods, rocker arms, and gears. The cylinder rods rose to a connection with rocker arms attached to the top of the boiler; these were connected to a set of vertical drive rods that propelled gears that engaged a single pair of driving wheels using a horizontal drive shaft. The up and down motion of these rods resembled the legs of a large mechanical grasshopper which is probably how the locomotive type got its name—Grasshopper. As specified by the B&O, the Atlantic burned anthracite coal (a hard, slow burning, but high-yield fuel). Draught needed for combustion was provided by an exhaust-steam driven mechanical blower.

Although it lacked the simplicity of the *Rocket*, the Atlantic was a success. Its small driving wheels, narrow wheel base, and low center of gravity were ideally suited to B&O's track structure, yet the locomotive was sufficiently powerful to move relatively heavy trains at speeds of 10 mph, and could even lift loads over graded sections previously thought too steep for locomotive propulsion. In 1833, Davis built another Grasshopper named Traveler. Sadly, Davis, like Shelley's mythical Dr. Frankenstein, was the victim of his own creation. He was accidentally killed when the locomotive he was riding on derailed.

Following Davis' untimely death, the B&O contracted Ross Winans and George Gillingham, who were closely affiliated with the railroad, to build locomotives, and provided them the use of their Mount Clare shops. Subsequent Grasshoppers featured a four-coupled design (giving power to all wheels), which proved more satisfactory than powering just one pair. The success of the Grasshopper led B&O to convert the bulk of its operation to steam haulage by 1835. By that time, the railroad had built 76 miles of line, and connected Baltimore with Harpers Ferry, MD. Locomotive historian Angus Sinclair estimated that 20 Grasshoppers were constructed, although not all of them were built for the B&O. The type remained in production until roughly 1837, when Winans advanced the design, replacing the vertical cylinders with horizontal ones. This new type is known as a "Coal Crab," or simply a "Crab." Winans continued to build and sell locomotives based upon this design of homegrown American technology for the next two decades.

It was the *Rocket*'s British-based technology that formed the basis for the vast majority of locomotives built in America and around the world, yet in the early years American locomotive technology had found a practical niche. Some Grasshoppers remained in service on the B&O for nearly six decades, where they worked at the Mt. Clare shops and on Baltimore terminal trackage. Here, their narrow wheelbase, and light axle loadings gave them an advantage over more contemporary designs. In later years, the locomotives were fitted with small cabs positioned at the front of the engine. Their historic value was recognized and several Grasshoppers have been preserved.

American Type

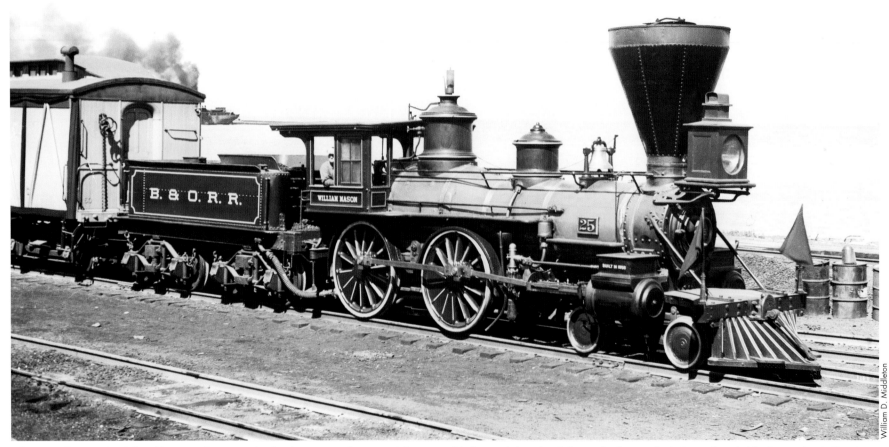

Baltimore & Ohio's No. 25 *William Mason* is a classic example of an American type locomotive. It features a tall balloon stack, large headlight, wooden "cow catcher" pilot, and is colorfully decorated in the Victorian style. The locomotive was manufactured in 1856 by Mason Machine Works, and it is seen here on display at the Chicago Railroad Fair in August 1948.

William D. Middleton

The American type is a ubiquitous symbol of 19th century American railroading. This common, well-balanced locomotive was found everywhere across the continent, working on a great variety of trains from slow branch line freights to fast mainline passenger runs. Not only was it the most prevalent locomotive type—more than 25,000 were built—but it was also one of the longest-lived types. The American type, or American Standard, is defined by its 4-4-0 wheel arrangement, which, using the Whyte system of classification, means the locomotive has four guiding wheels, four driving wheels, and no trailing wheels. In an earlier terminology it simply would have been described as an "Eight-Wheeler." Henry R. Campbell, chief engineer for the Philadelphia, Germantown & Norristown Railway, who patented the type in 1836, constructed the first 4-4-0. The type was modified a year or so later by locomotive builders, Eastwick and Harrison, who improved the locomotive's suspension system with the introduction of an equalization lever. This gave the 4-4-0 arrangement a three-point suspension, which was the key to the locomotive's success. The type's excellent suspension system, four-wheel leading truck, and its pair of driving wheels provided a flexible yet powerful machine with excellent tractive effort for its size. This combination was ideally suited for budding American railways that often had lightly-built tracks, where an agile and powerful locomotive had a distinct advantage over other types. The American type became popular during the 1840s and 1850s, just as the American railway network was rapidly expanding. The heyday of the 4-4-0 spanned the decades from the 1850s until the early 1880s, when locomotives were typically decorated with colorful Victorian flare. Brightly painted driving wheels, cabs and tenders, polished Russian boilerplates, tall balloon smokestacks, and lots of shining brass parts were the order of the day. Locomotive engineers of the time were assigned a specific locomotive and took great pride in its appearance and upkeep. This colorful era subsided when railroads in general switched from wood to coal fuel. The soot and grime from coal led many railroads to paint their locomotives with a dull, uniformly black paint.

The American type was never the domain of one builder, and the wheel arrangement was universally adopted by locomotive builders of the period. This did not mean all the locomotives were the same; on the contrary, there were numerous variations on the type. The size of the wheels and cylinders depended on the traffic a locomotive was designed to haul. Passenger 4-4-0s were built with tall driving wheels, sometimes as large as 80 inches in diameter. Large wheels were good for speed, while shorter wheels were better for moving heavy freight, where greater traction was required. Many 4-4-0s were built with moderately sized drivers and could be assigned without preference to freight or passenger traffic, as required. The size of the typical American grew enormously as the railroads required ever more powerful locomotives. Early 4-4-0s weighed only 12 to 15 tons, while late era machines weighed up to three times that amount. This reflected a general growth in the size and capacity of American railroad equipment.

By the 1880s, the American had lost favor as a freight locomotive, but the type continued to be built as a standard passenger locomotive until the mid-1890s, and after that remained in production for decades as a specialty locomotive. Despite its obsolescence and venerability, some 4-4-0s survived in service right to the end of regular North American steam operations.

An unusual example of an American type is Boston & Albany's *Berkshire*, a locomotive outfitted as an inspection vehicle. This beautiful engine was scrapped in 1929.

J.R. Quinn collection

John Gruber

Eureka & Palisade No. 4, the *Eureka*, is a wood-burning, three-foot gauge American type built by Baldwin in 1875. Now, *Eureka* is privately owned, but has occasionally run trips on preserved narrow-gauge lines in Colorado and New Mexico.

The *William Crooks* epitomizes the colorful look of a Victorian-era American type steam locomotive. It features a large "balloon" smoke stack, broad wooden "cow catcher," highly polished boilerplate, ornate ironwork, and a large headlight.

The 4-4-0 American type was a ubiquitous symbol of North American railroading during the later half of the 19th century. This locomotive was photographed at Southern Iron and Equipment Co., probably before it was either resold or cut up for scrap metal.

Photographer unknown, author's collection

20th Century Limited

Otto Perry, Denver Public Library Western History Department photo OP13610

New York Central's 1938 Dreyfuss-styled *Twentieth Century Limited* departs La Salle Street Station, Chicago behind a streamlined J-3a Hudson on August 10, 1939. This deluxe, extra-fare all-Pullman streamliner was considered the very zenith of American luxury rail travel.

In the thirty-five years since its demise, the *Twentieth Century Limited* remains one of the best-known trains in America. Originally known as just the *Twentieth Century*, it was the brain child of New York Central's George Daniels. It was inaugurated in June 1902, shortly after the dawn of the new century. At that time the "twentieth century" was the catch phrase of the day, just as the "millennium" has been used in modern times. The *Twentieth Century Limited* was just the railroad's latest gimmick.

Officially, Daniels held the position of general passenger agent, but he effectively assumed the role of the railroad's top publicity artist, a job at which he excelled. Today he is remembered for some of the greatest railway publicity stunts of all time. Daniels knew that fast trains caught public attention and he used the speed angle again and again to sell the Central's image. In 1893, he attracted worldwide attention with the run of New York Central's *Locomotive No. 999*. This specially designed American type made a well-orchestrated, lightning-fast run on Central's main line west of Batavia, New York. The date of this stunt just happened to be May 10, 1893, the 24th anniversary of the opening of the Transcontinental Railroad. The locomotive was reported to have hit the unbelievable speed of 112.5 mph! Since there were no proper speed recorders at that time, few people questioned the authenticity of this speed record until years later. In 1893, Central's *999* was a household word. That same year Daniels introduced the *Exposition Flyer* on a 20-hour schedule between New York and Chicago for Chicago's Columbian Exposition. Today, a 20-hour journey between New York and Chicago may seem tediously long, but in 1893 it was extraordinarily swift. It was so fast that the railroad couldn't justify it and it was quietly dropped after the close of the fair.

The New York Central and the Pennsylvania Railroad were long-time rivals—and the largest and busiest railroads in the United States competing with one another for freight and passenger traffic. Since the lucrative New York-Chicago passenger market was the most public manifestation of this fierce competition, it is no coincidence that both companies debuted fast, new New York-Chicago trains on the very same day. With the debut of the *Twentieth Century*, Daniels reintroduced the 20-hour schedule on the New York Central. Pennsylvania Railroad's *Pennsylvania Special* (which later became the *Broadway Limited*) also ran on an expedited schedule, and both trains were designed to compete for the top-end market. The mountainous Pennsylvania had a shorter, but more difficult route than the water-level New York Central. So while the *Twentieth Century* had to travel farther, it could travel faster than the *Pennsylvania Special*.

The *Twentieth Century*, as with most named trains, was a service, rather than a specific set of equipment (an important distinction that has eluded many travelers over the years). While the *Twentieth Century* operated with specially assigned, deluxe passenger cars, it was the extremely high quality service and fast schedule that made the train what it was, rather then the passenger cars and locomotives. In its heyday, the *Twentieth Century Limited* routinely operated in multiple sections. This meant

New York Central and Pennsylvania competed on many fronts, the most public of which was the lucrative New York to Chicago business passenger traffic. Central's *Twentieth Century* competed head-to-head with Pennsylvania's *Broadway Limited*; the latter is pictured here at Englewood, Illinois, in 1933.

J.R. Quinn collection

Richard Jay Solomon

New York Central's famous *Twentieth Century Limited* glints in the fading summer light as it races northward along the east bank of the Hudson River north of Cold Spring, New York. The fifteen-car train has just passed through the twin tunnels at Breakneck Ridge, a popular place for railway photographers over the years. This photo was made with a long telephoto lens from Storm King Mountain on the west side of the river.

there were two or more sets of equipment, each with its own locomotive and cars that ran as the *Twentieth Century*. Sections often operated on the same schedule, departing and following one right after another across the length of the railroad.

The *Twentieth Century* was never an ordinary train. It was marketed to the affluent traveler. Simply to have traveled on the *Twentieth Century* lent status to the individual. The train attracted a regular clientele, including the richest and most influential people of the day. The speed and comfort of this deluxe train has no true parallel today, although a comparison could be drawn between the *Twentieth Century* and the supersonic Concorde. The *Twentieth Century Limited* effectively ran non-stop between the New York and Chicago metro areas. In its heyday, after departing New York's Grand Central, it paused at Harmon, New York to change from electric to steam power, and then again at Englewood in suburban Chicago. The 20-hour schedule was gradually improved upon and eventually pared down to a 16-hour run. It was more than just a first class train, and required an "extra" supplement in addition to the first class fare. In the 1920s, the supplement alone cost each passenger $10, a considerable sum of money at the time. All passengers were treated to the finest Pullman sleeping cars—there were no "coach" seats. Passengers also had a variety of amenities not found on ordinary trains. There was a barber on board, a library, and baths. The original 1902 consists were equipped with electric lighting; at a time when the vast majority of American households did not have electricity, this was considered quite novel.

In 1938, New York Central and Pennsylvania each debuted new streamliners. Rather than relegate their once premier trains to secondary status in favor of all-new, flashy streamlined trains as had the Union Pacific, Burlington, and other Western Lines, the Central and Pennsylvania both worked with Pullman to design all new *Twentieth Century Limited* and *Broadway Limited* consists. The streamlined *Twentieth Century* of 1938 was one of the classiest trains to ever roll on American rails. The cars and locomotives were styled by Henry Dreyfuss and featured an elegant two-tone gray livery and powerful, specially streamlined J-3a Hudsons. The interiors were the epitome of art deco excellence, complete with diffused fluorescent lighting. After World War II, steam gave way to diesels, and New York Central used Electro-Motive E7s in the "lightning" stripe scheme to haul its flagship train. The "Century," as it would have been known to operating crews, was always a matter of company pride, and every effort was made to ensure its timeliness. Unlike so many of America's finest trains, the *Twentieth Century* was not allowed to deteriorate into a pathetic shadow of its former glory. Central operated it with dignity until shortly before its 1968 merger with the Pennsylvania. By contrast, the Pennsylvania's flagship *Broadway Limited* was gradually downgraded. The Broadway continued to operate as a coach and sleeper train well into the Amtrak era.

Richard Jay Soloman

In the summer of 1963, New York Central's New York bound *Twentieth Century Limited* rolls along the Hudson River at Manitou, New York. The splendid scenery of the lower Hudson Valley was the scenic highlight of the *Century's* run.

New York Central Hudson

The best-looking and most famous New York Central Hudsons were the last ten J-3a's, which had the Henry Dreyfuss streamlined treatment. New York Central J-3a 5450 was brand new when this photograph was made on April 17, 1938 at Croton-on-Hudson, New York—the northern extent of the Grand Central electrification on the Hudson Division. This streamlined Hudson is hauling a heavy-weight suburban consist, so it is most likely working a break-in run before being assigned to service on the *Twentieth Century Limited.*

J. R. Quinn collection

One of America's most famous and best performing steam locomotives was the New York Central's magnificent Hudson. This powerful, fast machine was named for the river along which it operated daily. In the 1920s, New York Central was America's penultimate passenger carrier, surpassed only by its archrival, the Pennsylvania Railroad. Burgeoning passenger traffic on its busy New York-Chicago route prompted the railroad's chief engineer, Paul Kiefer, to push the design of the six-coupled steam locomotive to its ultimate form: the 4-6-4 type. New York Central had obtained all it could out of its modern 4-6-2 Pacific types, so to get more power, Kiefer opted to adopt the four-wheel rear trailing truck, an innovation that had been introduced on the Berkshire type a few years earlier. This enlargement produced the 4-6-4 wheel arrangement, and allowed for a substantially larger firebox and boiler that would provide the locomotive with sufficient steam to maintain top track speeds with heavy consists for sustained periods of time. The first Hudsons were built by Alco in 1927, and featured a pleasing, well balanced, although straightforward, utilitarian appearance. Operationally, the Hudson was a fantastic success, allowing the railroad to expand the length of its trains, and reduce operating expenses.

In 1935, Kiefer set out to improve the Hudson by introducing a variety of refinements to the design. The result was the J-3a "Super Hudson." Among the changes, piston bore and stroke size were modified, operating boiler pressure was raised, lightweight alloy steel was used for reciprocating parts, while roller bearings were used on all locomotive and tender wheels. Also a new design of drive wheel was used in place of the conventional, spoked variety. The J-3a performed better than the earlier Hudsons, providing greater fuel efficiency, and also greater reliability.

The New York Central Hudson was a pioneering, streamlined steam locomotive. In 1934, Central equipped locomotive 5344 with experimental wind resistant shrouds in an effort to improved fuel efficiency. Later, Central applied different streamlining treatments to its Hudsons that were primarily aimed at improving the locomotive's appearance to make it seem more modern. No less than four different streamlining treatments were tried on the Hudson type. The most famous of these was a Henry Dreyfuss treatment initially applied to ten new J-3a's in 1938 in conjunction with the introduction of the new streamlined *Twentieth Century Limited*. For all its power, fame, and glory, the Hudson type succumbed to diesel power in the 1950s. New York Central management lacked nostalgic sympathies, so despite the great historical significance of its Hudsons, all were scrapped. However, other lines that had also adopted the Hudson did preserve examples, and these survive today.

The Hudson type was New York Central's standard mainline passenger locomotive through the late steam era. On April 30, 1950, J-1b 5224 Hudson leads the New York Express eastbound at Rensselaer, New York. New York Central's Hudsons were designed with a well-balanced, but utilitarian, appearance.

William B. Middleton

New York Central was the first, but not the last, North American railroad to develop the Hudson type. Canadian Pacific adopted the 4-6-4 Hudson type in 1929, just a couple years after the Central. CP's last 4-6-4's are its most famous. These semi-streamlined engines were known as Royal Hudsons because two of the class had hauled special trains carrying Britain's King George VI and Queen Elizabeth across Canada in 1939. Royal Hudsons were decorated with an embossed Royal crown, seen here on No. 2850 just above the cylinders.

Canadian Pacific photo, Richard Jay Solomon

23

The Gresley Pacifics

Courtesy Milepost 92 1/2

A Gresley A3 Pacific 60072 *Sunstar* leads an Edinburgh-to-London train at St. Margarets in Edinburgh in September 1957. The A3s were fast passenger locomotives regularly assigned to express trains on the former London & North Eastern Railway route between London Kings Cross, York, and Edinburgh, a line now known as the East Coast main line.

In the United States, development of steam locomotives using the 4-6-2 wheel arrangement followed a natural progression of locomotive evolution. The type melded the desirable qualities of the successful 4-4-2 Atlantic type and 4-6-0 Ten Wheeler, while overcoming suspension and tracking problems associated with 2-6-2 Prairies. The 4-6-2 uses a four-wheel leading truck, followed by three pairs of drive wheels, and a weight-bearing radial trailing-truck. The trailing truck is needed to support a large firebox that can provide the locomotive with enough steam to haul comparatively heavy passenger trains at relatively fast speeds. The combination of six large driving wheels and a large firebox was the key to the types' success. One of the first railways to use the 4-6-2 arrangement was Missouri Pacific, and it became known as a Pacific type.

The development of this large, powerful, fast locomotive coincided with a move toward significantly heavier and faster passenger trains. American railroads were moving away from all wooden passenger car construction, first with the introduction of steel framed cars, then (following several disastrous wrecks and fires), all steel passenger equipment. Steel cars were about a third heavier than comparable wooden cars, but passenger train weights also increased because the railroads were running longer trains to accommodate growing loads. Improved couplers and the perfection of the Westinghouse air brake in the decades prior to 1900 gave railroads the ability to run much longer trains than was possible in earlier years.

In the waning years of the 19th century, and the early years of the 20th, the 4-4-2 Atlantic type enjoyed a short reign as the most popular new type of fast passenger locomotive in America. By 1907, the Atlantic type was supplanted by the Pacific. Through the end of the Steam Era in the 1950s, the Pacific would remain the most popular type of fast passenger locomotive on American rails, though few were built after the introduction of the 4-6-4 Hudson type in the 1920s.

The British railways were much slower to adopt the Pacific; instead they were content to run passenger trains with smaller types for the first two decades of the 20th century. British passenger trains were much lighter than their American counterparts, and didn't require the same amount of pulling power. Passenger carriages, as they are known in Britain, tended to be much smaller than in America, in part because they had to conform to a more restrictive loading gauge and were neither as tall nor as wide as passenger cars on American lines. While British intercity passenger trains were generally not as long as those in America, trains in Britain tended to run more often. Other important considerations included differences in railway construction. American lines were known for prolonged grades, and in the West these often exceeded two percent (a rise of two feet for every hundred traveled; in Britain a two percent grade would be described as 1 in 50). By comparison, British lines did not have many prolonged gradients.

The 4-6-2 Pacific was properly introduced to Britain under the regime of Sir Nigel Gresley, the much-revered Chief Mechanical Officer of the London & North Eastern Railway (LNER). Under his expert guidance the type was refined

In a classic view of the last days of steam on the old LNER main line, in June 1962, A4 Pacific 60003 *Andrew K. McCosh* leads the 1605 (4:05 p.m.) departure from London Kings Cross to York at New Southgate in suburban London.

Courtesy Milepost 92 1/2

Courtesy Milepost 92 1/2

The streamlined class A4 Pacifics were one of the highlights of the late steam era. Their fast speeds, efficient performance, and distinctive streamlining have earned them a special place in the annals of world locomotives. In June 1955, A4 60015 *Quick Silver* races a northbound relief *Flying Scotsman* down Holloway Bank north of London. A "relief" train is the British term for an "extra sections"—an extra train run to nearly the same schedule as the regular name train in order accommodate heavy passenger loadings.

and perfected to a remarkably high standard. The Gresley Pacifics were some of the finest locomotives ever built, and among the highest achievements of more than 150 years of British steam power.

The East Coast main line has long been one of Britain's premier routes, connecting London's King Cross Station with Edinburgh in Scotland. The East Coast route came under control of the LNER as part of the Big Four grouping of 1923—a national consolidation that merged smaller railway companies into four

large, regional networks. Immediately prior to the official grouping, both the Great Northern Railway and the North Eastern Railway, two of the LNER components adopted the Pacific type to better accommodate the growing weight of passenger trains on the East Coast route. Gresley had designed the Class A1 Pacific for the Great Northern, while the North Eastern developed what is known as a Raven Pacific, later designated Class A2. The Gresley A1 quickly proved to be the superior of the two Pacifics.

The A1 Pacific used a "simple" three cylinder design, meaning that it was a single expansion engine, where all three cylinders operated with steam from the boiler, instead of the "compound" arrangement, whereby high pressure cylinders exhaust into low pressure cylinders. The A1 Pacific quickly demonstrated its merit and was highly regarded by the LNER, which regularly assigned the type to its best and fastest express trains, such as the *Flying Scotsman*, which ran from London to Edinburgh.

The best known of all the Gresley Pacifics, and certainly one of the most famous steam locomotives in the world is the *Flying Scotsman*. (This locomotive is often confused with the famous passenger train of the same name; the locomotive is a piece of equipment, while the train was a daily service.) Built as an A1 Pacific, the *Flying Scotsman* was the third Pacific to leave the Doncaster Works, and was originally numbered 1472 (it was later renumbered 4472, which is how it is best known). Its fame in Britain stemmed from its connection with its namesake train, which it occasionally hauled, and also from a widely publicized test run in 1934 when it exceeded 100 mph. Its fame grew in later years when it became a popular mainline excursion locomotive, and eventually toured both the United States and Australia.

Better Pacific Designs

In 1925, the LNER and Great Western Railway participated in a celebrated locomotive exchange, lending each other examples of their finest modern passenger locomotives for comparison tests. The results of this exchange surprised many observers, particularly those on the LNER. Instead of developing the Pacific type as LNER had, the Great Western had chosen to refine the traditional 4-6-0, and build its highly respected "Castle Class." As a result of the exchange, it was found that the Castle performed better on the LNER lines than the Gresley A1 Pacific! On analysis, the Castle demonstrated faster running and better fuel consumption on comparative trips. This must have been an embarrassment to Gresley and the LNER forces at the time, but resulted in further refinement of the Gresley Pacific—and ultimately produced a better-performing locomotive.

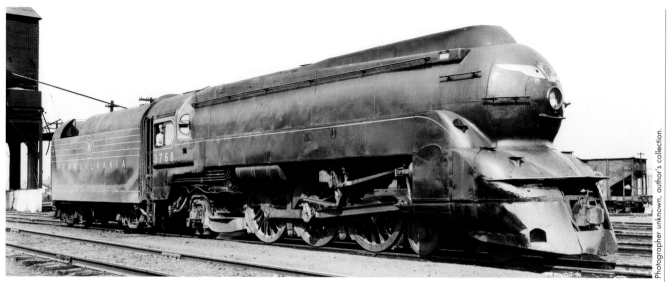

Photographer unknown, author's collection.

The Pacific type was a standard passenger locomotive on American railways. One of the best and most famous examples of the Pacific was Pennsylvania Railroad's class K4s (the small 's' indicating a superheated boiler). In the 1930s, PRR dressed up a few K4s in streamlined shrouds designed by Raymond Loewy. Streamlined K4s 3768 is seen at East St. Louis on April 2, 1946.

Fred Matthews

Perhaps the most famous locomotive of all time is the Gresley A3 Pacific 4472 *Flying Scotsman*. Not only is this locomotive a household name in Britain, but it is well known for its extensive touring in the United States and in Australia. Fred Matthews photographed the *Flying Scotsman* at Newcastle Central in 1967.

A detail of London & North Eastern Railway's A3 Pacific *Flying Scotsman*, a locomotive often confused with the passenger train of the same name. One is a steam locomotive (in other words a piece of hardware), while the other was a service that connected London and Scotland.

Gresley experimented with the Pacific type by raising boiler pressure, improving valve motion, and reducing cylinder diameter. Raising the operating pressure of the boiler gives steam more expansive energy, and thus more power. In order to withstand higher pressure, the boiler needs appropriate strengthening. Fine-tuning valve motion is crucially important to locomotive performance, yet is one of the elements of steam locomotive operation that is least understood. The valves and valve gear are machinery used to regulate the flow of steam to and from the cylinders. Conceptually, valve gear serves a similar function on a steam locomotive that a manual transmission does on an automobile. By adjusting the valves, a locomotive engineer (or driver, as he would be known in Britain) controls the speed, power, and direction of the locomotive. As the piston moves back and forth in the cylinder, the valves can limit the entry of the steam over a portion of the stroke. The point at which the flow of steam is stopped is known as the cutoff. Limiting the input of steam is called "shortening the cutoff." When executed properly, shortening the cutoff will reduce backpressure on the cylinders, and lower fuel consumption because less steam is required; therefore less water needs to be heated and less coal burned. This is what Gresley did on the two A1s following his experience with the Great Western Castles. By fine-tuning the valve motion, it was possible to save a few pounds of coal per mile. Over the course of a long run this savings added up, and when multiplied by a great number of locomotives over the course of a year, a few pounds per mile became quite significant. Reducing the cylinder size, even slightly, combined with a higher operating pressure also reduced fuel consumption. A drawback of smaller cylinder diameter was a reduction in the amount of starting tractive effort, which meant that it might be more difficult to start a train. This was in part overcome by using higher-pressure steam.

It wasn't just the cost savings that drove locomotive designers to improve fuel efficiency; it was a matter of great personal pride. Since the efficiency of a locomotive was a significant measure of locomotive performance, it was very important for a locomotive designer to build a machine with the best possible performance. Fast passenger locomotives were the railway equivalent of Formula 1 race cars, so having the best performing engines was something that railway managers strove to achieve.

Based on his experimentation, Gresley designed a new class of Pacific, designated Class A3 (the A2 designation had been assigned to the Raven Pacifics). While the A3 had the same basic proportions as the A1, it used a higher-pressure boiler (designed to operate at 220 psi, versus 180 psi on the A1s), and featured smaller cylinder diameters. The first of the A3 "Super Pacifics" was built in 1928, and over the next few years the LNER constructed 27 new A3s, giving it a fleet of 79 Pacific locomotives by the early 1930s. Eventually, the railway rebuilt the A1 Pacifics to A3 specifications.

Fast Trains and Streamlined Pacifics

In the early 1930s, new developments encouraged Gresley to further refine his Pacific design. For more than a generation, the minimum running time on the London-Glasgow and London-Edinburgh routes had been limited to 8 hours, 15 minutes. In 1932, this restriction was eliminated, and LNER trimmed 45 minutes from the *Flying Scotsman*'s sched-

Gresley's streamlined A4 *Mallard* holds the world speed record for steam. It reached a top speed of 126 mph in a well-documented run on July 3, 1938. While there are claims of other steam locomotives reaching such speeds and faster, none have proper documentation. *Mallard* is restored and beautifully displayed at the National Railway Museum in York, England. It is one of several A4s that have been preserved.

ule without any significant technological changes. Further, advent of high-speed diesel streamliners in Germany and America demonstrated the advantages and capabilities of high-speed trains. Intrigued by these developments, and anxious to introduce high speed trains to the LNER, Gresley asked the Germans to provide an estimated schedule for a *Flying Hamburger*-like streamliner on the London to Newcastle route. Unimpressed with the 4.5-hour German proposal, Gresley felt he could do better with steam and pushed forward a steam-powered streamliner. This required a new class of Pacific, designated A4.

The first A4 Pacific made its debut in 1935. Beneath the wind-resistant shrouds, the A4s were very closely related to Gresley's earlier designs. The A4 used slightly higher working boiler

pressure, featured redesigned steam passages to allow steam to reach the cylinders with greater efficiency, and used slightly smaller cylinders. In preparation for high-speed running, braking ability was improved and the suspension system modified.

The shrouds were designed using wind tunnel experiments carried out on models at the National Physical Laboratory. Aesthetics were entertained, as the shrouds were also made to look sleek and up-to-date in order to fulfill the public's perception of a modern, streamlined train.

On September 30, 1935, the LNER publicly debuted its *Silver Jubilee*, a sleek, fully streamlined, lightweight express train. It ran daily from Newcastle to London and back, taking just 4 hours to complete a 268-mile one-way jour-

ney. The train was so named to commemorate the 25th year of Britain's King George V. This new, fast train was an immediate public sensation.

The success of the A4 design led LNER to construct 35 of the class, the last one completed in 1938. When the 100th Pacific rolled out of the shops, it was named in honor of its designer, bearing the nameplate *Sir Nigel Gresley*.

Some of the Gresley Pacifics were equipped with special tenders that had a central corridor allowing engine crews access to the train. This very unusual feature, specially designed by Gresley, allowed for crew changes as the locomotive was moving, thus providing extra time savings on non-stop runs.

On July 3, 1938, Gresley staged a special run with one of his newest A4s, named *Mallard*—one of five specially modified A4s. The locomotive, attached to a few coaches and a dynamometer car, raced down the East Coast main line sustaining more than 120 mph for over 5 miles. It reached a top speed of 126 mph, thus shattering all world speed records for steam! To this date, *Mallard*'s achievement remains unsurpassed. While there are stories of other locomotives reaching such speeds, none have the verifiable record of the *Mallard*.

The advent of World War II put a close on Sir Nigel Gresley's Pacific development. In 1941, he died of a heart attack just short of his retirement. The Gresley Pacifics worked until the 1960s, when most were withdrawn and retired. Several have been preserved, and some are occasionally operated, including the famous *Flying Scotsman*, and the *Sir Nigel Gresley*. *Mallard*, the fastest of them all, is proudly displayed in all its glory at the National Railway Museum in York.

The arrival of a streamlined A4 Pacific was guaranteed to garner attention. In the early 1960s, after the A4s had been bumped from regular mainline service between London and Edinburgh, they held assignments in Scotland, such as the Glasgow-to-Perth runs. At Perth, Scotland, a group of boys thrilled at the sight of A4 60026 *Miles Beevor*, scramble to a view of the footplate.

Colin Garratt, Milepost 92 1/2

Germany's *Flying Hamburger*

German railway engineers had an early passion for the development of high-speed equipment. As early as 1903 Germany was setting speed records. That year, the Berlin-Zossen speed tests yielded an electrically powered car that achieved a top speed of 130.5 mph. (210 km/h). Experiments with streamlining led to the building of the Schienenzeppelin, the famous "Rail Zeppelin" in 1930. This curious-looking propeller-powered railcar easily reached speeds in excess of 100 mph, and on one occasion this car is said to have hit 143 mph (230 km/h). Although fast, this vehicle wasn't practical for regular service, and the concept was abandoned.

The desire for a more practical high speed train led to the construction of the world's first high speed diesel train. In 1932, Wagen und Maschinenbau AG built a streamlined, two segment-articulated, diesel-electric rail car. It was powered by a pair of 12-cylinder, 410 hp Maybach diesel engines. Although streamlining had become a popular industrial design style in the late-1920s, the primary impetus for this streamlining was based on the experience with the Rail Zeppelin, and was intended to reduce air drag and thus allow the train to travel faster. Wind tunnel experiments were conducted at the Zeppelin Works in Friedrichshafen. The diesel-electric streamliner underwent extensive testing before it was introduced into regular passenger service between Berlin and Hamburg on May 15, 1933. Named the Fliegende Hamburger, "The Flying Hamburger," the slick new train attracted worldwide attention as the fastest regularly scheduled train in the world. It covered a 178-mile (270 km) run in just 2 hours, 18 minutes—an average speed of 77.4 mph (125 km/h). To maintain this average, it operated at nearly 100 mph (160 km/h) for extended periods. This made it significantly faster than comparable steam schedules and produced a revolution in travel on Deutsche Reichsbahn (German State Railways).

Safety and speed must go hand in hand. To permit safe and fast running, the *Flying Hamburger* was specially equipped with advance braking systems, and the lines that it operated on were equipped with the latest advanced signaling systems including an early type of train stop that would automatically set the brakes if the train's driver passed a restrictive signal too quickly.

The immediate success of the *Fliegende Hamburger* prompted Deutsche Reichsbahn to order an additional 17 trains to establish the world's first high-speed railway network. High-speed rail travel was aimed at business travelers who would be able to accomplish long-distance, round trip travel in the course of a single day. Today business travelers take such schedules for granted, but at the time it was a bold concept, since most intercity business required at least an overnight stay. The diesel trains linked most major German cities. Thirteen of the high-speed diesel railcars were two-unit sets similar to the prototype, but equipped with fewer seats to provide travelers greater comfort. The remaining four trains were made up of three unit sets. Two of these used a hydraulic transmission system instead of an electric one. The hydraulic transmission set a significant precedent for later diesel locomotive development in Germany. To this day, Germany operates a sizeable fleet of diesel hydraulic locomotives.

In 1935, Deutsche Reichsbahn boasted the 12 fastest runs in the world, including a few that had average speeds nominally higher than that of the pioneering *Fliegende Hamburger*. These services were similarly named for the original train, carrying appellations such as the *Fliegende Kölner*, which served Köln (Cologne). The trains were enormously successful with the traveling public. The special services were discontinued with the advent of World War II, but many of the diesel railcars survived the war, and found use in the post-war environment running into the 1950s, on lines in both East and West Germany. Some of the cars have been preserved, and the original *Fliegende Hamburger* is displayed at the railway museum in Nürnberg.

Germany's *Fliegende Hamburger* "The Flying Hamburger" was a predecessor to successful high-speed diesel trains in the United States. The original two-car German streamliner debuted in 1932, two years before the Burlington *Zephyr*. A preserved, two-car *Flying Hamburger* train is seen at the Leipzig Hbf in June 2001.

Burlington *Zephyr*

Otto Perry, Denver Public Library Western History Department photo OP4705.

Burlington's *Zephyr* races across the plains of eastern Colorado. Based on the success of this train, Burlington bought a whole fleet of Budd-built stainless steel streamliners. In later years, the original train set, No. 9900, became known as the *Pioneer Zephyr*. It is now preserved at the Chicago Museum of Science and Industry.

The *Zephyr* was much more than just a new train–it was a fantastic publicity tool. Before the *Zephyr* entered regular service it was paraded around the country. It is seen in Chicago after it completed its record-speed run between Denver and Chicago on May 26, 1934. It made the run in just 13 hours and 5 minutes. By comparison, Amtrak's *California Zephyr* takes more than 20 hours to traverse the same route today.

Harry Rhoads, Denver Public Library Western History Department photo RH1132.

In the early 1930s, American railways were facing hard times. Automobile and airline competition combined with the economic downturn of the Great Depression had resulted in a precipitous drop in intercity rail ridership and, consequently, passenger revenues. In an effort to rekindle an interest in railway travel by sparking public imagination, two western railways took the initiative and sponsored the development of all new passenger trains along the lines of Germany's *Flying Hamburger*. These new trains melded emerging technologies with modern, streamlined styling to create a revolution in American railway travel.

During the 1920s, federally-sponsored research by the U.S. Navy resulted in the development of compact, high-output diesel engines. At the same time, new manufacturing techniques had emerged for the automated production of automobiles and commercial aircraft. Further, streamlining was in vogue with the public, while the fuel saving effects from lowered wind resistance had been demonstrated. The blending of these new ideas by Electro-Motive Corporation (a successful, gas-electric railcar manufacturer then recently acquired by automotive giant, General Motors) produced America's first streamliners. These modern, lightweight, wind-resistant passenger trains were powered by internal combustion engines which gave them great speed potential and minimized the need for service stops enroute.

Union Pacific's *Streamliner* debuted in February 1934, less than a year after Germany's *Flying Hamburger* had entered revenue service. UP's train was a three-piece articulated set featuring an aluminum riveted body assembled by Pullman (articulated railway cars are semi-permanently coupled, straddling a common set of wheels, instead of employing the conventional arrangement where each car has its own set of wheels

and independent coupler). It was powered by a Winton distillate engine and electric drive. (Winton was also a GM subsidiary, acquired in 1930 at the same time as EMC.) Although flashy, fast, and new, the *Streamliner* was, in a way, just a bigger, faster, and fancier motor vehicle. It was an evolutionary advancement of the product that Electro-Motive had been building (and Winton had been powering) for more than a decade. The *Streamliner* could easily reach 100 mph and was it a fantastic marketing tool! The train made numerous publicity runs and quickly caught the public eye, before entering revenue service as UP's *City of Salina* in Kansas. Arriving on the heels of this successful train was Burlington's *Zephyr*, which made its public debut on April 18, 1934. Conceptually similar to the *Streamliner*, the *Zephyr* embodied several important differences. Like the UP train, *Zephyr* was a three piece articulated set, built by EMC and powered by a Winton engine. Its body, however, was constructed by the Philadelphia-based Budd Company from stainless steel that was shot-welded in an automobile-like construction. Prior to the *Zephyr*, welded construction had been virtually unheard of on American railroads. The front end was a steeply pitched "shovel" nose vaguely resembling a medieval knight's polished helmet. The tail car featured a lounge with rear-facing windows allowing passengers to view the tracks passing behind them. But the *Zephyr*'s most significant attribute was its engine. Where UP's train used an older distillate engine, *Zephyr*

Burlington Route logo on the front of the *Pioneer Zephyr*.

was powered by one of Winton's first 201-A engines—a compact, two-cycle, high-output diesel engine. The *Zephyr* was America's first successful diesel passenger train and, like the *Streamliner* before it, the *Zephyr* made a public tour of the United States before entering revenue service.

The new trains thrilled hundreds of thousands. People flocked to see them pass at speed, took tours of their plush, new interiors, and of course paid to travel on them! The diesel streamliner caught on quickly, and within a few years both UP and Burlington were operating fleets of them. Numerous other lines had adopted the concept as well. The trains enjoyed great success and got people riding trains again. More important than

their short-term effect on ridership figures was the streamliner's long-term impact on the railroad industry. Unlike in Germany where the diesel streamliners, although successful, proved an operational anomaly, in the United States diesel streamliners prompted a diesel revolution that ultimately prevailed over the entire industry. Within two-and-a-half decades of the *Streamliner*'s debut, steam power had been effectively vanquished from American rails.

The welded stainless steel passenger car became a new American standard as well. Articulation as used on the early *Zephyr* trains was deemed inappropriate for regular operations, so later stainless steel cars were built with conventional types of wheel sets and couplers. The traditional "heavy weight" passenger car that had been the standard was effectively eclipsed by the *Zephyr*'s debut, and Budd became one of the leading producers of passenger equipment. Burlington's *Pioneer Zephyr*—as the train is now known—is beautifully preserved at the Chicago Museum of Science & Industry.

The *Pioneer Zephyr* was given a thorough cosmetic restoration at Northern Railcar in Milwaukee, Wisconsin during 1995 and 1996. The restoration crew poses with the historic *Zephyr* in April 1995. The train is now displayed at the Chicago Museum of Science and Industry. While the *Zephyr* now looks very much the way it did when released from Budd in 1934, it is now strictly a museum piece and is incapable of operation.

Milwaukee Road's *Hiawatha*

Photo by Otto Perry, Denver Public Library Western History Department photo OP5136.

Milwaukee Road's *Hiawatha* was the world's fastest regularly scheduled steam powered passenger train. Using shrouded 4-4-2 Atlantics, Milwaukee ran its trains at more than 110 mph on tangent sections. Today trains on the old Milwaukee Road are limited to just 79 mph, and they don't display any of the class or style that the art deco era *Hiawatha* embodied. Otto Perry caught 4-4-2 No. 1 leading a seven-car *Hiawatha* out of Chicago in the late 1930s.

New diesel streamliners were all the rage in 1934. Milwaukee Road viewed the diesel trains with great interest. Yet, while it liked the concept of a fast, flashy, new train, it wasn't sold on the diesel engine. It decided that the steam powered train could match the performance of Burlington's diesel *Zephyr*, yet using steam power would provide a more comfortable and more flexible train, and at less cost. So, the railroad's own Milwaukee, Wisconsin shops built a fleet of lightweight passenger equipment using conventionally coupled designs instead of the fixed, articulated consists used by the *Zephyr*, Union Pacific's *Streamliner*, and Germany's pioneering *Flying Hamburger*.

By using this more traditional approach, Milwaukee Road could tailor the make-up of its trains to match changes in ridership. So where Burling-ton and Union Pacific were saddled with the inflexibility of fixed-length trains, Milwaukee Road could easily expand capacity by adding a few more cars. Another advantage to this arrangement was the ability to substitute a locomotive if one failed. If one of the fixed-consist diesel trains suffered an engine failure, the whole train had to be taken out of service for repair.

At this time, the road diesel was still a few years away, and Milwaukee Road, like most railroads at that time, was still firmly committed to steam power. It ordered a small fleet of high-powered 4-4-2 Atlantic-type locomotives from Alco. These oil-fired machines had a large boiler capacity, operated at 300 lbs. psi, and featured 84-inch drivers, which were among the tallest driving wheels ever used by a locomotive in regular service in the United States.

Although very impressive from a mechanical perspective, technically these locomotives were just highly refined specimens of the same type of reciprocating steam locomotive used all over the United States. The one attribute that immediately set them apart was their flashy streamlined shrouds designed by Otto Kuhler. These locomotives were the very first steam powers delivered new with streamlined shrouding, although New York Central had earlier applied streamlining to one of its famous 4-6-4 Hudsons (see page 22). Using a wind tunnel, Kuhler had produced a *Zephyr*-like design in the art deco motif for Milwaukee's fast engines and new trains. Instead of painting them basic black, as were most steam power of the period, the new Atlantics were dressed in a more colorful scheme of light gray, with orange, maroon, and silver accents.

Milwaukee Road named its train *Hiawatha* after the legendary heroic Mohawk chief. The service was designed for the highly competitive Chicago-Milwaukee-Twin Cities corridor. The train debuted on May 29, 1935, just a little more than a year after Burlington's *Zephyr*. The *Hiawatha* quickly gained a reputation for its great speed. The locomotives were designed to operate at a sustained 100 mph, and in places needed to average more than that to keep to their rigorous schedule. They were capable of attaining at least 120 mph, and may have operated even faster than that in revenue service, making the *Hiawatha* the fastest scheduled steam powered train in the world.

The *Hiawatha* was an immediate success and Milwaukee's notion of flexible consists paid off. The trains quickly grew from five cars to nine, and a total of four Atlantics were needed to maintain the schedules. To allow for larger trains, Milwaukee ordered a fleet of high-powered 4-6-4 Hudsons that could haul more cars and maintain the fastest speed. Milwaukee Road gradually expanded its *Hiawatha* service to include a whole fleet of trains. In 1939, it introduced stylishly streamlined parlor-observation cars, nicknamed "Beaver Tails" because of their distinctive appearance. Then, after World War II, it built the famous "Skytop Lounge" observation cars that provided passengers with a unique tail-end panorama.

The super-fast steam era was remarkably short. Milwaukee started assigning diesels to the trains in 1941, and by the early 1950s the streamlined steam was done. Although the last Milwaukee *Hiawatha* operated in 1971, with the coming of Amtrak, Amtrak's trains today on the Chicago-Milwaukee route are again known by the *Hiawatha* name. Sadly, they are limited to a top speed of just 79 mph on the old Milwaukee route.

Graham, Jay Williams collection

In order to haul longer *Hiawatha* consists, Milwaukee Road ordered streamlined 4-6-4s from Alco. These locomotives were classed F7, and known on Milwaukee Road as "Baltics" rather than "Hudsons"; like the streamlined Atlantics, these 4-6-4s were designed for speed. Milwaukee Road F7 No. 100 was nearly new when photographed at St. Paul, Minnesota on October 29, 1938.

Pennsylvania Railroad GG1 Electric

Jim Shaughnessy

The GG1 was known for speed and power. On November 24, 1963, GG1 4879 races southbound on the Pennsylvania Railroad main line at Edison, New Jersey.

Richard Jay Solomon

Pennsylvania Railroad GG1 electric No. 4876 rolls westward through Rosemont, Pennsylvania, in suburban Philadelphia in the summer of 1963. Old 4876 is perhaps the most infamous of all GG1s. On January 15, 1953, No. 4876 leading the *Federal* from Boston to Washington, D.C., was involved in a spectacular accident when the train lost its brakes, careened out of control, and crashed through the bumper at Washington Terminal and smashed into the concourse of the station. No one was killed, but every newspaper in the country carried photos of 4876 amidst the wreckage of the station. Despite all that, this GG1 survived for another 30 years in service.

Pennsylvania Railroad's acclaimed GG1 was one of the most magnificent electric locomotives ever built—admired for its beautiful, well-balanced, streamlined appearance, its great power and high speeds, and its durability and longevity.

During the 1920s and 1930s, the Pennsylvania Railroad made the unprecedented move of electrifying the entire mainline operations on its heavily traveled routes between New York, Philadelphia, Baltimore, and Washington, D.C., and lines to Harrisburg. It was the most extensive project of its kind in the United States. PRR employed a high voltage overhead system that it had successfully applied to its Philadelphia suburban services beginning in 1913. Trains were powered from catenary energized at 11 kV single-phase alternating current.

Part of this extensive project was the development of a whole fleet of new electric motive power. PRR initially decided on a fleet of box cab electrics with rigid wheel arrangements that mimicked those employed by the line's most successful steam locomotives. Electric locomotive designations count axles instead of wheels, distinguishing powered axles with a letter designation. By the nature of their operation, electrics are bi-directional. PRR's class O1 electric was modeled after the 4-4-2 Atlantic type, and used a 2-B-2 wheel arrangement; the P5 was modeled after the railroad's very successful K4s 4-6-2 Pacific type (the "s" is part of the locomotive designation), and employed a 2-C-2 arrangement; while the L6 was an electric equivalent of the successful 2-8-2 L1 Mikado type and used 1-D-1 wheel arrangement.

While this practice of mimicking successful steam designs seemed logical, it soon proved flawed. The P5 developed several technical problems that forced PRR to re-examine its electric locomotive needs. Although the P5 was designed for high speed, according to an article in TRAINS Magazine, when traveling faster than 70 mph the locomotives suffered from severe lateral swaying. Also the axles were found to suffer from excessive cracking. While the locomotives were very powerful, PRR's operational demands were exceeding what a single P5 could accommodate, thus forcing the railroad to run two P5's in multiple on some trains. While this was not specifically a technology problem, it wasn't cost effective.

Another issue was crew safety. A P5 was involved in an accident that crushed a crew member in the cab, raising an issue on cab placement. The axles cracked because excessive torque was placed on them by the electric motors; this was solved by rebuilding the locomotives using larger axles. The lateral swaying and insufficient power problems proved more difficult to overcome. The Pennsylvania Railroad was legendary for its scientific approach to locomotive development and it attacked the problems with its electrics by experimenting with different locomotive wheel arrangements. A test track was set up at Claymont, Delaware, and between April 1933 and May 1934 the railroad analyzed different wheel arrangements in order to develop a locomotive that was single-handedly capable of hauling its heaviest passenger trains at high speed without suffering from lateral sway or other defect.

Among the locomotives it tested was a borrowed New Haven Railroad model EP3 box cab electric that featured an articulated wheelbase in a 2-C+C-2 arrangement. The riding qualities of this locomotive were very attractive. In 1934, the PRR built two new prototype electrics, one based on the EP3 using the 2-C+C-2 arrangement termed class GG1, the other using a 2-D-2 arrangement on a rigid base and classed R1. Both locomotives had similar carbodies. Addressing the safety issue, the locomotives had bi-directional centered cabs, and they featured modern streamlined, riveted shrouds. Following extensive testing, the GG1 prevailed, and PRR ordered a fleet of them for its passenger service. To improve the GG1's appearance, the railroad hired French-born industrial designer Raymond Loewy to clean up the look of the locomotive. Loewy suggested a welded body in place of the riveted construction, refined the locomotive's exterior design, and dressed it in its famous Brunswick green-and-gold pinstriped livery. Between 1935 and 1943, the railroad acquired 138 GG1s, many of which were assembled at its Altoona, Pennsylvania shops. Production GG1s were 79 feet, 6 inches long, with 57-inch wheels, and weighed between 460,000 and 470,000 lbs.

The GG1 was indeed a powerful, fast machine. It provided continuous 4,620 hp, and could develop much higher

Seen at Ivy City Engine Terminal in Washington, D.C., on June 18, 1960, GG1s 4874 and 4905 display two common paint liveries applied to Pennsylvania GG1s. The classic five stripe "cat's whiskers" seen on 4874 was replaced by the simplified single-stripe scheme in the mid 1950s.

Jim Shaughnessy

horsepower for short periods of time, allowing for rapid acceleration even with long, heavy passenger trains. A GG1 could swiftly accelerate an 18-to-20-car passenger train to 90 mph, and it could easily cruise along at 100 mph without straining. In tests, GG1s were capable of reaching top speeds in excess of 125 mph. The locomotives provided the Pennsylvania Railroad and its successors with more than four decades of reliable service on the Northeast Corridor. For most of their careers, the GG1s handled the majority of intercity passenger traffic on the New York to Washington route. The P5s were largely assigned to freight traffic (some of the later models also received center cab streamlined bodies). In later years, as passenger traffic declined and the P5s reached retirement, some GG1s (including the prototype, No. 4800) were re-geared and assigned to freight service. By the early 1980s, after more than 40 years, the GG1s had finally reached the end of their service lives. Amtrak operated GG1s until 1981, when the new and very capable AEM-7s (see page 55) assumed long-distance duties on the Northeast Corridor. The last of the breed served NJ Transit on the New York-South Amboy leg of its New York & Long Branch suburban service until October 1983. Happily, more than a dozen GG1s have been preserved for static display around the country.

Richard Jay Solomon

Enola Yards on the west bank of the Susquehanna River opposite Harrisburg, Pennsylvania, was the western limit of Pennsylvania Railroad's mainline electrification. In later years PRR re-geared some GG1s for freight service. On July 5, 1958, 4847 has just been cleaned and shines in the summer sun.

Jim Shaughnessy

Prototype Pennsylvania GG1 No. 4800 leads a light power move near Edison, New Jersey. The prototype featured a traditional riveted skin, while production models used welded skin and benefited from Loewy's refined styling.

EMD's 567 Diesel

On a glorious July 5, 1987, Central Vermont GP9 leads the Palmer switcher across the "diamond" (CV's level crossing with Conrail's east-west former Boston & Albany route) at Palmer, Massachusetts. The flexibility of the GP9 permitted railroads to assign the locomotive to a great variety of services. Electro-Motive GPs were once one of the most common diesel-electric locomotives in North America. Today they are relatively rare.

The success of its early streamliners thrust General Motor's Electro-Motive Corporation into the forefront of diesel production. In 1935, the company opened its La Grange, Illinois, facility and, despite the poor state of the world economy during the Great Depression, established an innovative business model to sell their products to American railroads. Initially, they sold both diesel switchers and passenger locomotives.

Electro-Motive had built its reputation on delivering a high quality product. While its early streamliners had proven their merit on the rails, EMC and GM engineers realized that the engine that powered these trains, the Winton 201-A diesel, was inadequate. So in 1936, they set about designing a better diesel engine. What they came up with was the 567, an engine based on the Winton two-stroke diesel, but an entirely new design with significant changes and refinements. Where the 201-1 was an in-line engine, the 567 used a "vee" configuration. The 567 design used larger cylinders, each with 567 cubic inch displacement—thus the model designation. The 567 revolutionized American railroads. Its essential design was the power plant for thousands of Electro-Motive diesels built over the next two-and-a-half decades, and it was responsible, more than any other engine, for the elimination of steam power on North American railways.

In 1938, EMC debuted the 567 engine on its E series passenger diesels, replacing the Winton 201-A used by earlier E models. Each new E-unit was equipped with a pair of 12-cylinder 567's that generated a total of 1,800 hp. A year later, in November 1939, EMC introduced one of the most significant locomotives of all time—its four-unit, freight locomotive, designated FT. Each of the four units was powered by a sin-

gle 16-cylinder 567 engine that generated 1,350 hp for a total output of 5,400 hp. The FT demonstrator set, a brown-and-cream colored locomotive number 103, was sent on an historic tour of American railroads where it clearly demonstrated the capability of Electro-

The familiar roar of EMD 567 diesels resonate along Oregon's Rogue River as a pair of venerable Southern Pacific SD9s work over the Siskiyou Line toward Grants Pass with a train of lumber from Medford on May 10, 1990. Southern Pacific preferred six-motor SD9s on its branch line local freights.

Motive diesels as serious freight hauling machines. Up until the FT, diesel locomotives had been something of a sideshow to traditional steam power. Yes, diesels had found a limited application as yard switchers in big cities, and as streamliner power plants, but throughout the 1930s, most of the real

work was handled by steam power. Once railroads saw what the FT could do on the road, they were quick to order them in large numbers.

The onset of World War II had dramatic effects on American railroads and on locomotive production in the United States. The war placed unprecedented demands on the railroads to move both freight and passengers, while simultaneously resulting in severe restrictions on the railroads' ability to acquire new locomotives. To maximize the use of resources, the federal government placed limits on manufacturers, regulating the

types of locomotives they could produce, and severely restricting the implementation of new designs. Diesel engines and electrical equipment were given first priority to military applications, so railroads were encouraged to use steam locomotives. In the short term, this benefited the large steam builders—Baldwin, Alco, and Lima—because the restrictions on copper and other materials needed for the war greatly limited the number of FTs Electro-Motive could sell (in January 1941, the EMC became the Electro-Motive Division of EMD). However this restrictive climate also enabled EMD to perfect its designs without serious concerns of marketplace competition from other diesel builders. Alco and Baldwin were allowed to build diesel switchers, but discouraged from selling road diesels, although both manufacturers drew up road diesel plans pending the lifting of the war-time restrictions.

By the time the war ended, American railroads had been sold on the advantages of diesel power and quickly began implementing comprehensive plans for dieselization. America was the first large nation in the world to abandon steam power, and did so at a very rapid pace. In this ravenous market for new diesel power, EMD was the clear market leader. Not only did its road diesels greatly outsell those of its competitors—Alco, Baldwin, and diesel engine manufacturer-turned-locomotive-builder Fairbanks-Morse—but EMD's road diesel set market standards that the other builders were to emulate. Yet, while these builders followed the engineering patterns set by EMD locomotive designs, they failed to copy EMD's successful market strategy.

EMD's market strategy was essentially an adaptation of the simple and straightforward policy that parent GM had used selling automobiles. It offered a few standard models that used standardized and interchangeable primary components, while maintaining design compatibility between locomotives even as models were upgraded. By doing this, it reduced the cost of engineering per locomotive, and improved reliability by limiting the number of changes per locomotive type. The result was that EMD locomotives had excellent reliability, while providing above-average performance. While EMD's competitors tried to pitch locomotives with slightly better performance characteristics, their reliability generally paled to that of EMD locomotives. In the long run, EMD locomotives outsold and outlasted the competition's. Where many Baldwin and Fairbanks-Morse diesels barely survived the steam-to-diesel transition period, EMD's continued to run for decades.

In the postwar market, EMD offered three basic model categories that accounted for the vast majority of its production. These were the E-unit, F-unit, and switchers. Like the prewar E's, the postwar E-unit was a streamlined dual-engine locomotive with an A1A-A1A wheel arrangement (A1A = three-axle truck where the center axle is un-powered) designed as a fast passenger road locomotive, while the F-unit was a streamlined road locomotive with a B-B wheel arrangement (two pairs of four axle trucks) for freight or passenger service. Switchers were smaller, lower horsepower locomotives designed for lightweight, relatively slow speed yard work. Where the E- and F-units featured handsome streamlining, the trademark "Bulldog" front end, and classy, colorful liveries, switchers were workhorses with well-balanced, but utilitarian, carbodies. All EMD's were powered by versions of the 567, ranging from 6 to

Richard Jay Solomon

One of the more unusual Electro-Motive models to use the 567 diesel was the BL2, which was one of the builders' early attempts at a road switcher type. In 1948 and 1949, EMD built 58 BL2s and a single BL1 for American railroads. Internally they were very similar to EMD's F3 road diesel. In the early 1960s, Rock Island BL2 429 leads a Chicago area suburban passenger train at Blue Island.

16 cylinders. New models were introduced every few years that reflected technological improvements, and resulted in greater reliability and improved performance.

By 1949, the diesel had vanquished steam in the new locomotive market. Except for the Norfolk & Western, which continued to build its own steam locomotive, every American railroad was ordering new diesels. Furthermore, almost every line in North America (with only a few exceptions, such as Alco-stronghold Delaware & Hudson), had purchased at least some EMD locomotives. The sounds of the 567 engine could be heard from New England to California and from Florida to Alaska.

One change in EMD's marketing strategy was to adopt a type promoted by its competition: the road switcher. Alco had introduced the road switcher type with its model RS-1 prior to American involvement in World War II, and after the war all the diesel manufacturers had started selling them. While EMD had dabbled with the road switchers, building models such as the BL2, in the immediate postwar environment it had focused on its three basic models. EMD's first serious road switcher was the GP7 (GP standing for General Purpose), a 1,500 hp machine that was mechanically the same as its latest F-unit model, the F7. The road switcher represented a victory of utilitarian design over industrial aesthetics. It didn't take long before EMD road switchers were outselling the F-unit that had been its most popular model type. The attraction to the "ugly" road switcher is not difficult to understand. They were cheaper to buy, easier and cheaper to maintain, and more versatile than the F-unit. Every road switcher was, by the nature of its design, a bi-directional locomotive and thus did not require turning facili-

Richard Jay Solomon

The "bull dog" nose of EMD's E- and F-units typified American railroad operations in the two decades after World War II. This 1960s view depicts FP7As on both Rock Island, and Chicago & Eastern Illinois. While Electro-Motive built 2,261 F7s for domestic use between 1949 and 1953, it only built 297 FP7As for domestic service. The FP7A was four feet longer than the F7A in order to accommodate steam generator water tanks for use in passenger service.

ties, and could be operated either singly or in multiples without any special considerations. The ability to string as many road switchers together as needed, without concern for which direction the cab was facing made this type especially appealing as railroads had found the traditional A-B-B-A configuration of the cab units operationally constraining.

By the mid 1950s, F-unit and E-unit sales were waning. EMD's most popular locomotive of the period was the GP9. Not only was the GP9 slightly more powerful than the GP7, but this model, along with the F9 and E9 introduced simultaneously, featured a variety of significant improvements over earlier EMD designs. The output of the 567 engine had been boosted to 1,750 hp by increasing the operating speed to 835 rpm, a new traction motor was introduced, and the locomotives were equipped with automatic wheel-slip correction providing improved traction. The success of the GP9 demolished any remaining resistance to EMD diesels. With the GP9, Norfolk & Western finally abandoned its all-steam policy, despite its perfection of the steam locomotives, and the new model effectively forced the weaker competitors, Baldwin and Fairbanks-Morse, right out of the locomotive market.

Expanding upon the four-axle, four-motor road switcher, EMD also introduced a six-axle, six-motor road switcher. Its first such model was the SD7 (SD stood for Special Duty), and later the SD9: both models corresponding to the GP7 and GP9. Although the six-motor concept only attracted nominal interest in the 1950s, the six-motor EMD would eventually become the best-selling locomotive type in America.

By the early 1960s, EMD had boosted the output of the 567 engine,

A trio of EMD E7 diesels leads one of Burlington's *Zephyrs* at Chicago Union Station. The early *Zephyrs* employed fixed consists with shovel-nose stainless steel power cars, while later *Zephyrs* used a more flexible arrangement with conventionally coupled stainless-steel passenger cars and regular production diesel-electric locomotives.

pushing the design to its limit with further increased rotational speed and the addition of a turbocharger. The 16 cylinder 567 engine finally capped out at 2,500 hp, nearly twice the output of the original 16 cylinder engines used on the FT. High output 567s were used in EMD's GP35s, SD35s, and even a few eight-axle monsters, designated DD35, built for Union Pacific and Southern Pacific. This was as far as EMD could push the engine, so the company decided to advance a new design based upon the success of 567. Thus EMD's 645 engine was born, and the era of new 567 locomotives came to a close. Yet even today, more than 35 years after the last 567 locomotive rolled out of La Grange, the sounds of the 567 can still be heard—and not just in America: EMD sold locomotives for export as well. Some of these were built in the USA, while others were built under license in a variety of countries overseas.

Left and Above: The last place in the United States where EMD F-units were regularly assigned in the traditional A-B-B-A configuration was on LTV Mining ore trains in northern Minnesota. This route was built in the mid 1950s to move iron ore from mines in the Iron Range to boats on Lake Superior. In 2001, the line shut down after more than 40 years of operation.

Richard Jay Solomon

Left: On the afternoon of August 25, 1959, a pair of Reading Company FP7s led the *Crusader* out of the Central Railroad of New Jersey's Jersey City terminal. The skyline of lower Manhattan is clearly visible beyond the terminal on the other side of the Hudson.

Right: The unusual nature of the dual mode FL9 prolonged its service life as a mainline locomotive. A pair of Metro-North FL9s led a Poughkeepsie-bound commuter train near Cold Spring, New York on September 4, 1997, more than 40 years after the type was introduced.

Talgo

Richard Jay Solomon

Rock Island's TALGO was powered by an Electro-Motive LWT12 locomotive (which used a 12 cylinder 567C diesel engine). Three LWT12 locomotives were built. This train was built for service as the *Jet Rocket*; the other two powered General Motors' *Aerotrain*. Lightweight trains did not enjoy great success in the United States, and by the early 1960s Rock Island's TALGOs, along with both *Aerotrains,* were working the Rock's Chicago suburban services, a big step down from the prestigious long-distance services for which they were intended.

Low-slung TALGO passenger equipment has carried passengers for more than half a century. These unusual, but significant trains have an interesting international history. Today these trains regularly operate in Spain, Germany, and the United States—three countries, as it happens, that have all produced important components for the trains over the years.

The TALGO concept was the genius of Spanish inventor Alejandro G. Omar, whose name is incorporated in the TALGO acronym. According to an article on TALGO in October 2001, *Today's Railways*, the name originally stood for "Tren Alejandro Goicoechea," however this meaning was later modified to reflect the train's articulated design and include Omar's business partner, José Luis de Oriol y Urigüen, and thereafter TALGO stood for "Tren Articulado Ligero Goicoechea-Oriol." Omar conceived of the TALGO concept in the late 1930s, and developed it in the 1940s.

There are several key elements that distinguish TALGOs from traditional designs. Instead of conventional construction, TALGO passenger car bodies use a very lightweight tubular design. The cars are coupled together in a fixed articulated set, known as a "rake" (articulated railway cars are semi-permanently coupled and straddle a common set of wheels instead of the conventional arrangement where each car has its own set of wheels). They ride on specially designed wheel pairs in the place of conventional swiveling "trucks" or "bogies" found on the vast majority of railway equipment. The elimination of the four-wheel swiveling truck was designed to reduce wheel wear and permit a low-profile, low center-of-gravity train capable of relatively high speeds. Indeed, a TALGO train is immediately distinguished by its low profile. The

American Car & Foundry built several TALGOs under license in the United States. Some trains were sent to Spain for regular service, but one train was intended for demonstration purposes in America. On July 23, 1954, the American TALGO demonstrator was on display at Springfield, Massachusetts. This train was eventually sent to Spain where it was re-gauged for 5 foot 6 inch track and placed in revenue service.

Donald Shaw, Robert A. Buck collection

cars generally measure slightly less than 11 feet above the rail, which is a third lower than typical Continental and American passenger cars. The cars are shorter in length, as well.

In the mid 1940s, following the construction and demonstration of a prototype in Spain, TALGO contracted American Car & Foundry (ACF) to construct several train sets. Three were built for Red Nacional de los Ferrocarriles Españoles (RENFE-Spanish National Railways), and a demonstrator was built to promote in the United States. In 1954, ACF sent its train on a tour of American railways hoping to generate sales for the new design. At the time, several American railways had expressed renewed interest in fast, lightweight train designs as a way of boosting passenger revenues which had dropped off dramatically following the conclusion of World War II.

Twenty years earlier, the debut of Union Pacific's *Streamliner* and Burlington's *Zephyr* (see pages 31-34) had spurred the public interest and resulted in the construction of dozens of new trains that helped revitalize the industry. So in the mid 1950s, some of America's largest passenger carriers invested in a variety of new, lightweight trains including the *Aerotrain*, New York Central's *Train-X*, and a tubular train on the Pennsylvania Railroad, hoping to again rekindle public enthusiasm for passenger travel. In 1957 and 1958, the Boston & Maine, New Haven, and the Rock Island debuted ACF-built TALGO trains. The B&M and NH powered their trains with streamlined Fairbanks-Morse diesel locomotives, while the Rock used one of General Motors Electro-Motive Division's futuristic-looking LWT12 diesels —the same model used to power GM's

own *Aerotrain*. Unlike the diesel streamliners of the 1930s, the 1950s lightweights failed to satisfy the public's transportation needs. By the late 1950s, Americans were abandoning railroad passenger services at alarming rates as new interstate highways were built and airline services improved. Within a couple years of their debut the lightweight streamliners were withdrawn from service, while railroads carried on with more conventional equipment.

TALGO had vastly more successful experiences in its native Spain. The early production trains debuted in 1950 on RENFE's Madrid to Irún run, at the northern border of France. For Spanish passengers who had not enjoyed the streamliner era in the 1930s, the TALGO was a real treat. These trains were much nicer than the traditional, old Spanish passenger trains. In addition to quicker schedules, according to *Today's Railways*, the Spanish TALGOs were the first air-conditioned trains in Europe. The success of TALGO led RENFE to introduce additional TALGO services and order a new fleet of trains. To power these new TALGOs, very powerful diesel-hydraulic locomotives, designed by German locomotive builder Krauss-Maffei, were ordered and built under license in Spain. Like the passenger cars, these locomotives were built with a low profile and low center of gravity. Additional diesel-hydraulics were ordered from K-M in 1969 and again in 1982, as RENFE continued to expand the scope of its TALGO services.

Over the years, TALGO has produced numerous innovations to its basic design. Most Spanish railways were built as broad gauge. The tracks are 5 feet 6 inches wide, compared to the standard 4 feet 8.5 inches used by most railways in Europe and America. This gauge discrepancy complicates international rail travel beyond the Iberian Peninsula (Portugal uses the same broad gauge as Spain); passengers have been forced to change trains at the border. In the late 1960s, TALGO invented a variable-gauge axle that permitted its train to switch from one gauge to another while moving at a slow speed, thus allowing them to operate directly into France and beyond. In 1969, through services began between Madrid and Geneva, Switzerland (although since trimmed back to just a Madrid to Montpellier, France run). The gauge changing system found another important market with the opening of the Spanish high-speed line in 1992, a route known as the Alta Velocidad Española or AVE. This all-new route connects Madrid and Seville via Cordoba. It was built in the French model and hosts TGV-style high-speed trains that can run at speeds up to 186 mph (300 km/h). Unlike the rest of the RENFE mainline network, the AVE route uses 4 feet 8.5 inches standard gauge. Although the AVE route is effectively isolated, it is anticipated to eventually connect with the rest of the European network. Despite domestic gauge incongruities, special gauge changing TALGOs, designed for 125 mph (200 km/h) operation, permit through domestic services over the AVE line. In 1980, TALGO introduced a tilting variant, known as TALGO pendular. This employs a passive tilting system that allows the train to operate faster through curves without passengers feeling the ill effects of centrifugal forces. Today, TALGO pendular trains operate on a variety of routes including the AVE line. Presently, TALGO is working on the next generation of trains, which have been tested at speeds of 217 mph (350 km/h) and faster. Both electric and diesel powered designs are being developed.

TALGO generated renewed interest in the United States following the importation of a pendular demonstrator in 1988. Although this train was originally considered for the North East Corridor between Boston, New York, and Washington, Amtrak ultimately bought TALGOs for operation in the Pacific Northwest. The first of these trains entered regular service in 1994. A second TALGO made a widely publicized American tour in 1996. Additional trains were acquired, and today pendular TALGOs regularly operate in *Cascades* services between Eugene, Oregon; Seattle, Washington; and Vancouver, British Columbia. TALGO also found a market in Germany where pendular sleeping-car trains are in regular service.

Amtrak operates several TALGO pendular sets in *Cascades'* service in the Pacific Northwest.

A few of the 1960s era TALGO III sets were still in regular service on RENFE in 2001. These trains have fluted sides resembling other streamlined lightweight equipment from the period. While the early TALGOs featured single wheel-set articulated cars and a low center of gravity design, they did not use pendular tilting technology that was developed later.

One of most significant technological advances of the TALGO design is its patented independent wheel sets that are used in place of conventional swiveling twin axle trucks. A detailed view of an Amtrak TALGO pendular for *Cascades'* service shows the single wheel between two articulated cars.

One of RENFE's high-speed T-200 TALGOs races toward Cordoba on the AVE line against the backdrop of the castle and village at Almodóvar del Rio. The T-200 is a gauge-changing pendular TALGO that is designed to work through services that use both 5 foot 6 inch gauge and 4 foot 8.5 inch tracks. The locomotive leading the TALGO is derived from the German class 120. While intended for TALGO service on the high-speed route, it is not part of the articulated train set.

Germany's Class 103 Electric

An aged Class 103 electric basks in the fading sun of a beautiful summer day at Bonn, Germany with an InterCity train bound for Köln. The heyday of the streamlined Class 103 has come and gone. While a few of these electrics remain, they have been largely replaced by more modern locomotives on traditionally-run trains. More to the point, Germany is moving away from traditional consists in favor of modern articulated trains such as the ICE.

In the 1960s, Deutsche Bundesbahn (Germany Federal Railway) planned to develop high-speed services on several core routes. The rekindled interest in high-speed operation in Germany resulted in the development of a new, fast, and powerful class of electric locomotives, rather than the pursuit of high-speed diesel trains along the lines of the *Flying Hamburger* (see page 30). Prototype locomotives designated E03 were built in 1965, and designed to lift a 300 ton (approximately 661,521 lbs or 331 short tons) train up a 0.5 percent grade at a maximum speed of 125 mph. Furthermore, the E03s were capable of very rapid acceleration and needed just 2.5 minutes to reach maximum speed. They employed a welded, streamlined design based on wind tunnel tests; the frame supported a five-section body comprised of the two-end driving cabs and three machinery compartments, of which the center compartment was the largest. Contrary to conventional high-speed electric design in Europe, these locomotives used a six axle C-C wheel arrangement instead of a B-B arrangement. The six-axle, six-motor arrangement allowed for smaller traction motors and distributed the weight of the locomotive better than a four-axle machine. One of traditional drawbacks of a six-axle design is inferior tracking ability, which seems to have been overcome with the German prototype.

Deutsche Bundesbahn (DB) operated a high-speed demonstration service between Munich and Augsburg in 1965, and for a few years operated a regular deluxe train service at 125 mph. However, significantly greater costs of operating passenger trains at 125 mph caused DB to scale back its ambitions for a few years, and settled for 100 mph operations until 1977, when 125 mph speeds were resumed. After five years of testing and discussion, a fleet of locomotives based on the E03 entered regular production. These are known in modern DB parlance as the Class 103. In the standard DB classification numbering system, each locomotive is identified by the class number followed by a unit number; for example: 103.199. Like the prototypes, production Class 103s were painted in an attractive variation of the red-and-cream livery used by the deluxe international Trans-Europ Express (TEE) trains.

The Class 103 was the first type of locomotive in Germany equipped to operate with an advanced continuous cab signaling system. This system was designed to provide greater protection when operating at high speeds by giving the locomotive driver earlier warning or restrictive signals. This also allows for automatic speed control, which permits the locomotive driver (engineer) to set the speed of the locomotive, which will then automatically accelerate and maintain that speed regardless of the effects of the gradient, yet staying within the limitations imposed by signaling.

By 1977, DB had made sufficient investment in infrastructure and signaling improvements to raise its speed limit on some lines to 125 mph. In 1979, DB increased the lengths of its trains, allowing it to finally take full advantage of the Class 103s speed and power potential. Most of the class were rated at roughly 8,000 hp continuous output, and could produce as much as 12,000 hp for short durations in order to accel-

A classic maroon-and-cream painted Class 103 electric rolls through Düsseldorf in August of 1998. The 103 was designed as a fast, powerful electric, capable of rapidly accelerating long passenger trains to a speed of 125 mph.

erate trains quickly. Rapid acceleration was as important, if not more so, than the locomotive's ability to maintain high speed, because of the types of services Class 103s worked. Since many German passenger trains make relatively frequent stops, and the profiles of many DB lines do not permit long stretches of maximum speed, it is important to reach maximum speed as quickly as possible in order to make the best advantage of fast trains.

For more than two decades the Class 103 led many of Germany's finest and fastest conventional passenger trains. Today, Germany is one of the leaders in high-speed rail transport, and it oper-ates a network of fast trains that connects many of its largest cities. The construction of new high-speed lines has greatly improved long-distance services. The re-unification of Germany in 1991 resulted in a renewed emphasis on east-west transport. While modern streamlined InterCity Express (ICE) trains now operate on the fastest schedules, there are still many locomotive-hauled trains operating at a 125 mph top speed. The Class 103 has survived, and as of this writing in 2001, a few remain in regular service, while others are held as reserve locomotives to cover assignments in the event another locomotive, or even an ICE train fails.

On May 24, 1996, DB Class 103-146-7 leads an InterCity train at the Köln Hbf (Cologne's main railway station). This locomotive is still wearing the classic maroon-and-cream livery that was designed to match the Trans Europ Express trains.

In the afternoon of May 24, 1996, a Class 103 electric speeds an InterCity passenger train northward along the Rhein at Namedy, Germany. This once heavily traveled route will lose many of its through-trains with the opening of a new high-speed line between Köln and Frankfurt. The new line doesn't follow the scenic, circuitous, water-level profile of the Rhein, but instead runs inland over the mountains.

A Class 103 electric at Berlin in June 2000. By this late date, the Class 103 only had a few regular assignments.

A DB Class 103 electric whisks a southbound InterCity train through Bonn, Germany, in August 1998.

Swedish Class Rc Electrics

On December 21, 1992—the winter solstice—an Amtrak AEM-7 rolls across the Susquehanna River at Havre de Grace, Maryland, against the backdrop of the rising sun.

The Swedish Rc electrics were the first commercially produced locomotives to use thyristors for motor control. In June 1998, a Statens Järnvägar (the Swedish national railway) Rc-6 leads a passenger train in Stockholm. Swedish railways are largely electrified using a high voltage overhead system energized at 15kV, 16.6Hz, the same as in Germany, Austria, and Switzerland.

The world's most prolific electric locomotive designs are those derived from the Class Rc developed in Sweden in the mid 1960s. More than 2,000 locomotives have been built based on the Rc design, and they operate on railways everywhere from their native Sweden, and Scandinavian neighbor Norway, to Austria, Bulgaria, Croatia, Iran, Romania, and the United States.

The Rc was developed by Allmänna Svenska Elektriska Aktiebolaget (ASEA), a company that later became part of ABB. The first locomotives entered service on Statens Järnvägar (SJ, the Swedish national railway) in 1967. The Rc was the first mass-produced locomotive to use thyristor motor control. A thyristor is a semi-conductor, and thyristor motor control is used in place of traditional electro-mechanical or pneumatic controls. Thyristor control has several distinct advantages over the older systems. It enables step-less traction motor control, which maximizes motor output but minimizes wheel slip, thus creating a more powerful, efficient locomotive with greater tractive effort, while requiring less maintenance.

Over the course of three decades, 366 electric locomotives based on the pioneer Rc design entered revenue service on SJ. Based on roster information printed in *Today's Railways* and other sources, these included 20 Rc-1s, 100 Rc-2s, 10 Rc-3s, 130 Rc-4s, and Rc-5s and Rc-6s, as well as a freight service locomotive designated Rm, with slow speed gearing designed to haul heavy iron ore trains north of the Arctic Circle. The Rm electrics have also been used in freight service elsewhere in Sweden. Rc electrics are bi-directional, featuring an attractive, although utilitarian, double-ended body design. They are relatively short compared to many modern locomotives, use a standard B-B wheel arrangement, and draw power from overhead catenary. In Sweden, the overhead wires are energized at 15kV, 16.6Hz. Most of the original Rc's were designed to produce 4,555 hp continuously.

American interest in the Swedish electrics started in the mid 1970s when Amtrak was searching for an effective replacement for its former Pennsylvania Railroad GG1 fleet (see pages 36 to 39). It tested an Rc-4 on its electrified Northeast Corridor, and viewed the powerful electric favorably. Under license, General Motors built a variant of the Rc for Amtrak, designated the AEM-7. The AEM-7 has a stronger body shell than the Rc to meet American safety requirements, and the AEM-7 locomotive is significantly more powerful in order to reach higher speeds in revenue service. Amtrak's AEM-7s produce a continuous 5,695 hp, and regularly operate at speeds up to 125 mph (200 km/h). By comparison, SJ's original Rc was designed for 84 mph (135 km/h), while later models, such as the Rc-3, were geared for 100 mph (160 km/h). Amtrak's first AEM-7s entered service in 1980 and have been the primary locomotive on the Washington-New York-New Haven Northeast Corridor route ever since. With the completion of the electrification extension between New Haven and Boston in 2000, Amtrak's AEM-7s began hauling regular, scheduled trains on the full length of the Boston-Washington run, eliminating the need for the traditional New Haven engine change. Three commuter rail operators followed Amtrak's lead in acquiring electrics based on the Swedish Rc: NJ Transit, Pennsylvania's SEPTA, and Maryland's MARC use their electrics in push-pull suburban passenger services around New York, Philadelphia, Baltimore, and Washington. While SEPTA's and MARC's locomotives share the AEM-7 designation with Amtrak's locomotives, NJ Transit uses ALP-44s that were built by ABB and its successor, Adtranz.

The Swedish national railway SJ uses class Rc in both passenger and freight service. On a gray June afternoon, SJ Rc-2 No. 1111 leads a freight through Stockholm.

Amtrak's AEM-7 is an adaptation of the Swedish Rc electric design. Since 1980, AEM-7s have been a common sight on the Northeast Corridor between Washington, D.C., New York City, and New Haven, Connecticut. In November 1995, AEM-7 942 pokes out of the B&P Tunnels in Baltimore, Maryland.

Amtrak AEM-7 electrics No. 907 leads a northbound train through the curves at Elizabeth, New Jersey, on August 1, 1986.

A Statens Järnvägar Rc-2 leads a short passenger consist at Stockholm Central. The Rc electric was developed by ASEA in the 1960s. It was the first commercially-built locomotive to use thyristor motor control.

The Success of the HST

Colin Garratt, Milepost 92 1/2

In the 1970s, the HST gave British Rail the tool it needed to substantially improve its intercity trains services all across Britain without implementing major changes to the existing infrastructure. The HST, operated as the InterCity 125, provided frequent, fast, comfortable train service to passengers for the same price as existing trains. The trains were a total success, as the public responded and ridership climbed dramatically.

In the 1930s, British railways were setting world records with their high-speed operations, as demonstrated by Sir Nigel Gresley and his fast Pacifics. Unfortunately, World War II had disastrous implications for British railways and their operations. After the war, British Railways did not resume the level of service they had offered in the 1930s, and service gradually declined further through the 1950s. In the face of a hostile political climate and intense and growing competition from air and highway transport, British intercity passenger rail travel was following the American path to near oblivion by the 1960s. Long-haul passenger services simply couldn't compete with other modes, and British Railways, by this time a nationalized transport network, had to take action or accept that its intercity services were forever doomed.

American railways had faced a similar situation in the postwar environment and had reacted by buying new, deluxe diesel-powered streamliners in an effort to offer improved services. One of the failings of this approach was that while the streamliners offered comfort and prestigious luxury travel, they were not fast enough and did not offer sufficiently frequent schedules to compete with private automobiles or commercial airline services. Americans were sold on the automobile because of convenience, and traveled by plane because of speed; for the most part American railways provided neither convenience nor speed, and ultimately exited the passenger business, allowing the government to run Amtrak as a skeletal intercity service beginning in 1971. Amtrak has been most successful on the routes, such as the Northeast Corridor, where it provides fast and frequent services, and can compete with both autos and airplanes.

Virgin Cross Country is one of five post-privatization franchises that operate HST sets in Britain. In July 2001, a Virgin HST rolls through Hinksey Yard in Oxford. All HST trains use a push-pull arrangement with Class 43 streamlined diesels at both ends of the train.

During the 1960s, British Railways initiated a draconian scaling back of its operations, abandoning thousands of route miles and closing hundreds of stations. However, it also made a concerted effort to improve services on selected key routes. On the East Coast main line (between London King's Cross Station, York, and Edinburgh), 100 mph diesel-hauled trains debuted in 1962 using the fabled "Deltic" locomotives. This service cut the running time between the English and Scottish capitals to just 6 hours. An even more ambitious plan was implemented on the West Coast main line route between London Euston station, Birmingham, Liverpool, and Manchester. This route was upgraded and electrified allowing for fast and frequent services between these important British cities—a move that proved an unqualified success. Within just a few years of electrification the ridership on the West Coast route had doubled, and was one of the most heavily traveled intercity railways in the world. Clearly the combination of speed and frequency was the key to boosting ridership on intercity lines.

Enter the HST

In the late 1960s, there were two schools of thought about expanding British Rail's high-speed passenger network. One group promoted the concept of an Advanced Passenger Train (APT), a thoroughly redesigned train that would permit speeds of up to 150 mph on conventional lines using advanced propulsion systems and tilting carriages (to minimize the unpleasant effects of centrifugal forces on passengers). The other group pushed forward the development of a High Speed Train (HST) that employed conventional railway technology using diesel-electric propulsion and used newly designed (but not radically advanced or tilting) passenger carriages to provide 125 mph service on existing lines. Both train systems were developed simultaneously in the early 1970s. While the APT had a more ambitious goal of providing much faster service, the HST was ready for revenue service much sooner because it employed more proven technology.

Less than two years after the HST was authorized in 1970, a prototype was ready for testing. On each end of the seven-car train was a wedge-nose diesel-electric locomotive in a push-pull arrangement. Each locomotive was powered by a high rpm Valenta-Paxman 12-cylinder diesel capable of generating 2,250 hp. This provided the train with 4,500 hp, which gave it the very high power-to-weight ratio needed for rapid acceleration and maintaining high speeds.

Getting a train up to 125 mph and keeping it at that speed was only part of the HST design challenge; more important than reaching 125 mph is stopping safely from that speed. Since the whole concept of these fast trains was that they should operate at high speed over existing lines and not require specialized rights-of-way (as in France and Germany), they needed to be able to stop as quickly as conventional trains. This meant the HST needed to be able to slow from 125 mph to a full stop in just 6,600 feet in order to work within limitations established by existing signaling. To achieve this, the HST's designers adopted electro-pneumatic disc brakes on all wheels, combined with protective equipment to prevent over-braking that might cause wheel slide or other damage. This was the first major use of the disc brake in Britain and provided the HST with more effective braking than conventional, slower-moving trains.

The HST used the newly designed Mk3 passenger carriage, a design that had been underway prior to the authorization of the HST, and was adapted to the HST configuration. The Mk3 employed a monocoque body design that was very strong and lightweight. Measuring 75 feet, the Mk3 was longer than any previous design. Often specialized equipment results in incompatibility problems, but this was not an issue with the HST because the trains were intended as semi-permanently coupled sets and would not need to couple with any other type of carriages in regular service. Since comfort and ride quality were paramount concerns, every effort was made to ensure passengers would receive a smooth ride at speed. In addition, the cars were all air-conditioned and featured large, sealed windows.

Although the HST had its share of political hurdles to overcome, including labor concerns, it quickly proved itself to be technologically sound and it was easily capable of reaching 125 mph. On one occasion a special HST running north of York on the East Coast main line reached a top speed of 143 mph. This milestone is important to British engineers who have a history of achieving world speed records, and this made the HST by far the world's fastest diesel-electric.

HST Debut

British Railways didn't hesitate to take advantage of the HST's potential. Initially, a fleet of 27 production train sets was built for service on the old Great Western Railway main line west

A First Great Western HST crosses a tall stone arch viaduct at Liskeard on its way from Penzance to London Paddington on April 2, 2000.

from London Paddington. This route was Isambard K. Brunel's acclaimed "Billiard table," a level, tangent railway, designed for "high speed" service (roughly 60 mph) back in the 1830s, and for this reason had been built to Brunel's legendary 7-foot gauge. The Great Western connected London with Reading, Swindon, Bristol, and cities in south Wales. Although the route was ideal for high-speed operation, minor infrastructure adjustments were required before 125 mph service could begin. Some restrictive curves were eased, and drainage was improved. More importantly, the signaling was upgraded to give HST drivers additional warning in advance of junctions and switches at 125 mph.

The trains were marketed as the Intercity 125, a name obviously joined to the HST's high-speed ability. The most successful aspect of the HST development, and where BR really scored a

coup, was how they used the trains. Where the old school might have ordered just a few trains to offer a handful of premier high speed services, BR introduced a *full* service of high speed trains on the lines west of Paddington. The Intercity 125 was not just fast, new, clean, and more comfortable than older trains, but operated frequently and did not cost any more to ride. When the full HST schedule was in service, there were some 48 daily Intercity 125s. This was exactly the sort of convenience needed to lure people from their cars, and the strategy worked. Another impressive feature of the HST service was that BR managed the intensive HST schedule on the existing infrastructure while simultaneously accommodating a high volume of existing freight and passenger traffic on the route. This is a remarkable achievement, considering that some Intercity 125 schedules were matching the station-to-station running

times provided by the Japanese Shinkansen, which was afforded an exclusive right of way. By 1979, a few Intercity 125 runs had achieved an average speed of 111.3 mph between station stops which, for a short time, made them not only the fastest, regularly scheduled diesel trains in the world, but also the fastest scheduled trains! While the French TGV and later Japanese trains would soon set new records, the HST had made its mark.

The enormous commercial success of the Intercity 125 on the former Great Western lines prompted British Railways to expand the service, and in March 1978, it introduced the HST to the East Coast main line between London Kings Cross and Edinburgh. For this service 32 new HSTs were built. These trains used eight car sets instead of seven, as the twin power cars were deemed sufficiently powerful to accommodate the weight of an extra passenger carriage. British Railways had ordered 42 sets of equipment for this route but were constrained by budget cuts. The HST was a success in this corridor as well, and soon BR was ordering more trains for additional routes. Cross country Intercity 125 service between the Northeast and Southwest was inaugurated in 1979, and eventually the service was expanded, so that Intercity 125s connected most major cities in Britain. The Intercity 125 reached from Inverness and Aberdeen in Scotland, to Southampton, and cities in Cornwall. By 1982, there were 95 HST sets in service, along with spare carriages and power cars. Although the HST trains were only capable of achieving maximum speeds on some lines, the HST allowed for BR to successfully develop and market the Intercity 125 network of fast, frequent passenger trains, thus giving BR the tools it needed to recapture and retain a significant portion of the intercity travel market.

In August 1979, a British Rail HST operating as the eastbound *Cornish Riviara Express* approaches Exeter St. David's station to the thrill of local train spotters gathered on the platform. The signal box and semaphores date from the steam era and present a wonderful technological contrast. The beauty of the HST is that it allowed British Rail to dramatically improve its long-distance services without a massive investment in upgrading its physical plant.

Fred Matthews

The HST Today

In the 1990s, the British railway network underwent a radical transformation. The system was divided into different units, and then returned to the private sector using an unconventional and highly controversial plan. Instead of selling the tracks and infrastructure to competing companies, the railway infrastructure was sold to one company, and railway service franchises to more than 25 different companies. This bold experiment in railway privatization has had mixed results and has been the subject of continual discussion in the British media ever since. In late 2001, Railtrack plc (the company in charge of railway infrastructure) went bankrupt, causing a scandal that has put the whole privatization scheme under intense public scrutiny.

Several of the passenger franchises acquired intercity routes, and as a result there are now five different franchises using HST sets. Richard Branson's Virgin operates both the West Coast main line and intercity cross-country services, known as Virgin West Coast and Virgin Cross Country respectively. Virgin trains are painted in the company's trademark red-and-black livery, with bright yellow ends for safety. Midland Mainline, which operates the old Midland route north from London St. Pancras to Leicester, Derby, and Sheffield, inherited a small fleet of HSTs. Although the hill-and-dale Midland route does not allow the HSTs to make the best of their speed, the trains are used to provide an excellent hourly service on the route. The Great North Eastern Railway (GNER) operates the East Coast main line franchise. When the East Coast route was electrified all the way to Edinburgh in the early

1990s, many of the HSTs assigned to the route were re-deployed elsewhere. However, a few HSTs were retained for services that reached beyond Edinburgh. Since GNER now operates some of these routes it has a handful of HST sets that are painted in its attractive deep blue-and-red-livery. By far the largest and most intensive operator of HSTs is First Great Western, which, as one might expect, operates over many of the old Great Western Railway lines

west from Paddington. First Great Western's green, white, and yellow HSTs are used on the same routes that BR first deployed the HST on more than 25 years ago.

In 2001, the privately run franchises began deploying new high-speed intercity trains that will both augment and replace runs handled by the HSTs. Yet as of this writing in late 2001, it was recently reported in *Modern Railways* that some HSTs were working up to 1,100

miles a day. Not bad for an old train that still reaches its top speed of 125 mph without straining. The train that saved British intercity passenger services still carries millions of passengers every year, and still has some miles left in it despite a quarter-century of intensive service.

Britain's East Coast main line was a choice route for HST services until the line was completely electrified between London King Cross and Edinburgh in the early 1990s. As of this writing in 2002, GNER was the primary long-distance operator on the ECML, and the majority of its trains are electrically powered. A few runs, however, such as those that continue beyond the end of electrification at Edinburgh, still use 1970s era HST sets. In December 1999, a GNER HST races through York.

Milepost 92 1/2

Top left: The success of the HST in Britain led to the export of the powercar technology to Australia in 1981. Initially marketed as the InterCity XPT (standing for Express Passenger Train) these trains served several routes radiating outward from Sydney in New South Wales. While the power cars are very similar to those used by British Rail, the passenger cars are an Australian design and look quite different from the Mk3s in Britain. This photograph, made on September 29, 2000, shows one of the Australian trains in the Countrylink livery.

Above: The HST earned the title of the fastest diesel trains in the world. Its engines roaring, a First Great Western HST races past Pilning toward the Severn Tunnel on July 16, 2001.

Left: First Great Western HSTs pass at Pilning near the east portal of the Severn Tunnel.

Section Two

RAILWAY TERMINALS & STATIONS

Leipzig Haupbahnhof.

Heuston Station Dublin

Dublin's Heuston Station is one of the oldest passenger terminals in the world in continuous use. It was designed in 1845 and opened in 1848. Today it hosts Iarnród Éireann (Irish Rail) as the primary terminal for long-distance trains serving the west of Ireland and some suburban services. The headhouse, pictured here, functions as railway offices. In earlier days, passengers were encouraged to use an entrance on the south side. Following a renovation in 1998, this façade became a main entrance to the station.

Dublin's Heuston Station is a railway terminal from the dawn of the railway age, yet still serves as one of the city's primary railway stations. It is among the oldest railway stations in continuous use in the world. Few stations have survived from the formative age of railways, and far fewer city terminals exist from this period.

Heuston is located near the Guinness Brewery along the south bank of the River Liffey, a little more than a mile west of Dublin's city center. Al-though the name sounds similar to London's Euston Station, there is no connection between the two. The Dublin terminal, formerly known as Kingsbridge, was renamed in 1966, along with many other stations in Ireland as a commemoration of the 50th anniversary of the Easter Rising. At this time, railway stations were renamed in honor of participants in the Rising who had been executed by British authorities in the aftermath of the event, so this station is named for Sean Heuston.

Heuston was the main passenger terminal for the Great Southern & Western Railway and designed in 1845 by Sancton Wood. This young British architect had considerable experience with railway structures and, according to an article in a 1975 issue of the *Irish Railway Record Society Journal*, also designed a number of other buildings along the GS&WR, including the stations at Portarlington, Portlaoise (formerly known as Maryborough), and Thurles, as well as part of the Inchicore Works (locomotive shops). Wood's Dublin terminal presents a decidedly different character than his other Irish stations, and exhibits a neo-classical motif consistent with other public and civic structures in Dublin, rather than the Victorian gothic themes that were preferred at rural locations. Heuston's headhouse is three stories tall, although it appears to be just two stories tall when viewed from the front. The lower story is dressed in stone blocks, while the second level features a Classical en-

Heuston Station, Dublin.

gaged Corinthian colonnade that rises to meet an ornately decorated cornice. The upper floor is used as office space, while the lower floor is for passengers. Two short decorative towers that lend pleasing symmetry to the frontal façade flank Heuston's main structure. Behind the headhouse is an iron shed covering roughly two-and-a-half acres of tracks and platforms, designed by the railway's chief engineer Sir John Macneill. Train sheds have a long history and this shed, like the station it serves, is among the oldest in the world still used as intended. (Isambard K. Brunel's shed at Bristol Temple Meads in England is older. It was built in 1841, and while still standing, is it no longer used to cover active tracks.) Kingsbridge station was opened in 1848, and after more than 150 years, is still one of Dublin's main train stations.

The station's exterior has changed very little over the years, but much of the interior bears little resemblance to its original design. It has been renovated and rebuilt several times over the years, most recently in 1998. Today, passengers may enter directly through the front of the building; this space was once an office, and passengers were encouraged to enter by the southern entrance leading to the booking hall. The booking hall itself features a period clerestory ceiling and traditional ornate molding. By today's standards, Heuston Station is a modest facility, especially when compared to the big London terminals or busy stations on the Conti-nent. Yet the station accommodates dozens of passenger trains daily. As of this writing, Heuston's present operator, Iarnród Éireann (Irish Rail), has ambitious expansion plans to increase capacity through the addition of more tracks and platforms. A new light-rail system is also being built in front of the station that will allow easy connections for passengers traveling to Connolly Station, the city center, or the south-westerly suburb of Tallaght.

The primary passenger entrance to Heuston station was this one, located on the southern flank of the building complex. Like many city terminals of the period, Heuston station uses classical architectural elements such as engaged colonnades and arches.

St. Pancras Station London

The vast St. Pancras balloon shed is the work of William Barlow. It spans 240 feet, and rises to 100 feet above the rails. Its skylights were blocked up during World War II to protect the station when Axis bombs rained down nightly on London. Soon this pioneering shed will be renovated and should regain much of its Victorian era appearance, despite a modern extension that will be erected beyond the end of the traditional span. Here, St. Pancras is seen in July 1999; a Midland Mainline Class 170 is on the right, and one of the company's HST sets on the right.

The importance of London as both Britain's largest city and the seat of government resulted in a multitude of railway lines radiating from it in every direction. Each line was built and originally operated by a different company and, as a result, each had its own London terminal. Despite the later consolidation and eventual nationalization of the British railway network, London still boasts more than a dozen major termini, several of which are among the most famous in the world. Victoria, Paddington, and Waterloo stations are undoubtedly familiar names, made famous through literature, film, and advertising references. Readers of Harry Potter will be familiar with the terminal at Kings Cross, where the magical *Hogwarts Express* departs from the imaginary Platform 9-3/4. However, the greatest London railway terminal, and perhaps one of the finest stations in Britain, is St. Pancras station, which was built by the Midland Railway between 1865 and 1876. This grand station is located in central London facing Euston Road, and adjacent to the station at Kings Cross.

St. Pancras is by no means the most important London terminal in regards to the traffic it has handled—in 1904 it accommodated only 150 trains per day, a relatively small number compared to London's busiest stations. What makes it significant is its remarkable and influential architecture. The station's great balloon arch train shed, the very first of its kind, spans 240 feet, measures 689 feet long, and rises to 100 feet above rail level at its peak. It was designed by the Midland's engineer, William Barlow, who wanted to keep the space below track level available as storage facilities, and thus wished to keep it free from a complicated network of shed supports that would have been required for a typical multi-span shed of the period. The broad, open space below the shed provided passengers with a dry environment in which to board trains, while the tall and ventilated roof permitted locomotive smoke to escape.

The details of the shed design were worked out by R. M. Ordish, a roof and bridge engineer, and the Butterley Company of Derbyshire constructed the shed. To this day, if one inspects the shed's supports, one will find the Butterley name cast in iron. The St. Pancras terminal was opened in October 1868, although the most famous element of the station, its magnificent headhouse and hotel, was not completed for another eight years.

It is the Midland Grand Hotel, designed by Sir George Gilbert Scott—one of London's best-remembered 19th century architects—that has made St. Pancras famous in the eyes of most travelers. This enormous, ornate brick and stone building exemplifies the secular Victorian Gothic architectural style of the period. The hotel's 565-foot frontal façade, and exquisitely executed clock tower, 270 feet tall, completely conceal the vast shed, platforms, tracks, and trains behind it. Arriving at St. Pancras on the street, in a taxi or on foot, one may wonder if the building is a railway station at all! But of course, it is. In addition to necessary railway facilities,

St. Pancras is anything but an ordinary railway station. The Midland Grand Hotel is the St. Pancras headhouse, and this magnificent Victorian Gothic building housed booking offices, waiting rooms, and baggage facilities in addition to one of London's finest late 19th century hotels. In the 1930s the hotel was closed and the space converted to railway offices.

such as booking offices and waiting rooms, the building originally housed a 500-room hotel that, in its heyday, was deemed among London's finest accommodations. By 1935, the hotel fortunes had waned, and the space was converted to company offices.

Barlow's great balloon shed inspired a whole generation of similar structures in Britain, on the Continent, and in America. Commodore Vanderbilt's original Grand Central Depot in New York City once sported a balloon shed much like St. Pancras'. The largest balloon shed in the world, which spanned 300 feet, was at the Pennsylvania Railroad's Philadelphia Broad Street Station. Of the great balloon sheds built in America, all were eventually demolished, except for that at Philadelphia's Reading Terminal, which has survived, albeit not as a train shed, but today as a convention center and shopping plaza.

Despite efforts to convert or demolish it, St. Pancras Station remains a railway terminal, and the public can still admire both its train shed and headhouse. With the privatization of British Rail in the mid 1990s, St. Pancras became the terminal for the Midland Mainline franchise and hosts the company's white and aqua HSTs (see pages 58 to 61) and Class 170 Turbostars. Unfortunately, the shed has lost some of its former glory as the many skylights designed to brighten the station were covered over during World War II in answer to the German bombing blitz against London. Sadly, the shed has become a cavernous, gloomy place to board trains. But this grand old terminal will not be left to languish much longer. St. Pancras is to become the new international terminal for the *Eurostar*, (see pages 156 to 157), and the station will be rebuilt and renovated in conjunction with the construction of the Channel Tunnel Rail Link—new high-speed lines linking London with the west portal of the Channel Tunnel at Folkstone. While the facilities will be modernized, the traditional balloon train shed will be restored to its appearance in the late Victorian Period. The skylights will be renewed and ironwork painted a sky blue. Unfortunately, the traditional shed is not long enough to accommodate the 18-car long *Eurostar* trains, so an additional shed is to be constructed beyond Barlow's balloon structure. Artist impressions and models of the new shed reveal that it will be built using a modern architectural style that seems entirely incongruous compared with the historic architecture. Ironically, the renovation will give St. Pancras a renewed status as one of London's important railway terminals, but the station's character will be forever altered in the process.

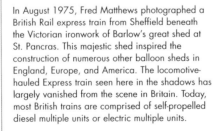

In August 1975, Fred Matthews photographed a British Rail express train from Sheffield beneath the Victorian ironwork of Barlow's great shed at St. Pancras. This majestic shed inspired the construction of numerous other balloon sheds in England, Europe, and America. The locomotive-hauled Express train seen here in the shadows has largely vanished from the scene in Britain. Today, most British trains are comprised of self-propelled diesel multiple units or electric multiple units.

Fred Matthews

This view of St. Pancras in July 2001, shows the Barlow balloon shed and the back of the Midland Grand Hotel. At the time the station was opened in the mid 1870s, the vastly different styles between the "modern" iron shed and the Gothic hotel were considered a great architectural contrast. Today they seem like a natural combination, yet the planned improvements to St. Pancras using present day construction techniques and styles may seem grossly out of place by comparison with the Victorian architecture.

Washington Union Station

Washington Union Station is one of America's finest railroad terminals. The station's beaux-arts design borrowed elements from classical Roman architecture.

One of America's finest railway terminals can be found in the nation's capital, Washington, D.C. Here, a beautiful beaux-arts station sits resplendent in a city renowned for its finely planned layout and wonderful neo-classical architecture. It hasn't always been this way. Back in 1900, Washington, D.C. suffered from badly designed railway stations that neither matched the stature of the surrounding architecture, nor provided adequate transportation facilities. Two stations, both of which failed to serve the needs of travelers, then served the city. The inspiration to build the present day Union Station came about during an effort to improve the city along the lines illuminated by the original plan laid out by L'Enfant in 1789. In 1902, the new station was planned, and its design was executed by Daniel H. Burnham and Company. Burnham was well known for his design of the 1893 Columbia Exhibition in Chicago, and the Pennsylvania Railroad's station in Pittsburgh, Pennsylvania.

Washington Union Station opened on October 27, 1907, and at that time it was the largest railroad station in America, if not the world. Its great concourse features a 760-foot long façade. When the station opened, its immense waiting room was 220 feet long, 130 feet wide, and covered by a great vaulted ceiling decorated with gold leaf, reaching to a height of 96 feet at its apex.

The whole terminal area, including the tracks and support facilities, occupied roughly 200 acres. Most of the station's tracks are stub-ended, while a few are depressed below street level, funneling together to reach a two-track tunnel that runs below Capitol Hill for services that continue beyond Washington to the south.

Washington Union borrows architectural elements from imperial Roman architecture, resembling an oversized Roman basilica. The station is decorated with 36 statues of Roman Legionnaires, the work of sculptor Augustus St. Gaudens. Students of railway architecture may notice striking similarities between Washington Union and New York's Pennsylvania Station (demolished in 1963). This is no coincidence. Daniel Burnham and Penn Station's architect Charles F. McKim were well acquainted with each other's work, and both architects were part of the team that planned the general improvement of Washington, D.C.

The station was originally owned by the Washington Union Terminal Company, which was jointly controlled by the Pennsylvania and the Baltimore & Ohio Railroads. Washington Union also served trains operated by the Southern, Chesapeake & Ohio, Richmond, Fredericksburg & Potomac, Seaboard Airline, and Atlantic Coast Line.

UNION STATION, CONCOURSE, WASHINGTON, D. C.

When Washington Union Station opened in 1907, its concourse was the largest room in the world under a single roof. It was 760 feet long and contained 110,200 square feet of floor space. This space has been substantially altered by station renovations over the years.

Washington Union has faced its fair share of troubles. On the morning of January 15, 1953, a few days before Eisenhower's inauguration, Pennsylvania Railroad's famed overnight Boston-Washington sleeper *Federal Express*, led by GG1 electric No. 4876, lost its air brakes on approach to the station. Traveling at high speed, the train crashed through the bumper at the end of Track 16, leveled a newspaper stand, and burst into the concourse. The floor quickly collapsed under the weight of the GG1, and the locomotive sank into the basement. Although no one was killed, the wreck was sensational and covered by every newspaper in the country. Both the station and the GG1 were quickly repaired.

In the 1960s, the Pennsylvania Railroad wished to demolish the station and develop the property in the same way that it had New York's Pennsylvania Station, but Congress intervened and stopped further destruction. Yet, during the 1970s, the station building suffered from neglect, as did most railway stations in the United States, and in 1981 it was closed to the public. Although demolition was again considered, sounder minds prevailed, and in 1988, following a multi-million dollar renovation, Washington Union Station reopened. In addition to its transportation facilities, the station now hosts a two-level shopping mall with 120 shops and restaurants. Today, it proudly serves Amtrak, Virginia Railway Express, and the Maryland rail commuter agency known as MARC. It is the southern terminus for Amtrak's deluxe high-speed *Acela Express*—America's fastest train, which debuted in December 2000.

Grand Central Terminal

This is how Grand Central's immense concourse appeared shortly after the station's recent renovation. During the day Grand Central is an extremely busy place, but by 10:20 p.m., when this photo was exposed, the station is mostly empty.

New York City's Grand Central Terminal is, perhaps, the finest of all railway masterpieces. Its world-class architecture, innovative engineering, and masterfully integrated civil design makes it not only among one of the greatest railway terminals, and one of the finest buildings in New York, but one of the best examples of early 20th century architecture.

Grand Central Terminal's unique fascination is a mixture of its beautifully executed beaux-arts architecture, its fabulously large grand concourse, and the enormous human traffic that it accommodates daily. Yet, its mystique lies in its vast subterranean network of tracks and interconnecting passages that reach into the depths of New York. Grand Central's less obvious passageways are a modern day troglodyte's paradise. Within the public terminal complex are dozens of shops, restaurants, bars, and public services; it was a precursor to today's enclosed shopping mall—the predominant American market place. But "The Terminal City," as the New York Central described its achievement on the eve of its opening in 1913, is truly a city within a city. Underground passages connect the terminal with many of the surrounding buildings, including hotels and office complexes. It was once said that tourists or businesspersons could arrive at Grand Central and entertain all of their needs and desires without once setting foot outside. Since most travelers, however, had agendas beyond the scope of the terminal, passengers were afforded the convenience of direct connection to the New York City subway system, with several routes converging on the station. Grand Central's legendary myriad underground rooms and passages was exploited in the first *Superman* film, which portrayed the villain Lex Luther

Sodium vapor lamps illuminate Grand Central's 42nd Street façade against the fading blue glow of a winter evening sky.

living in a secret part of its complex. While the movie was fantasy, it represented the labyrinthine qualities of the station (and, indeed, there *are* hidden rooms and passageways).

Integral to Grand Central Terminal's original success as a station was that, in addition to the subway trains, mainline trains arrived below ground, too. Mainline trains passed through a 2.5 mile-long tunnel below Park Avenue, which at 59th Street begins to fan out to 69 tracks on two levels below the streets of Manhattan.

The Upper Level platforms were designed for both long-distance and suburban services, and the lower level for mainline-suburban traffic. A separate set of seven tracks on the far west side of the Upper Level were designated as the long-distance arrival station, with a large, separate area for meeting arriving passengers. These tracks converge on a loop track, hidden below the main waiting room, which brought trains all the way around to the far eastern side of the station to head to the yards without having to reverse ends. They could then be serviced and backed into the terminal for their next run, with all seats pointed in the correct direction. The loop was duplicated on the lower level. Dual loops were built on this level, with the inner loop (no longer—because modern cars are too long to negotiate its curves) for suburban trains, and the outer loop for an additional arrival station, directly below the Upper Level arrival station, which was never completed and serves as a maintenance area today.

Grand Central was the first large, bi-level underground railway terminal in the world, and has remained the largest such facility. While other stations may be busier, none have as many tracks.

Grand Central Terminal's engineers have been widely praised for their clever civil engineering, exemplified by the station's efficient pedestrian traffic flow. The unprecedented use of wide ramps to direct passengers through the station, and the skillful separation of suburban and long-distance traffic, was one of the station's characteristic attributes.

The New Grand Central

The present day Grand Central Terminal was born in the early years of the 20th century, when New York City's explosive population growth strained the capacity of the old Grand Central Depot to the breaking point. The earlier station dated from 1869, when Commodore Vanderbilt combined the New York Central and the New York and Hudson River Railroads. Opened in 1871, the first Grand Central was also heralded as magnificent. It featured a vast balloon train shed modeled after London's St. Pancras (see pages 68 to 71), which had opened just a few years earlier. Although a large station for its day, the first Grand Central reached capacity within a generation, so it was substantially enlarged in 1899, only to be demolished a few years later to make room for the present building.

From its inception, Grand Central Depot served the trains of both the New York Central and New Haven railroads, which brought burgeoning suburban traffic in addition to considerable long-distance business. Although not yet the busiest American passenger terminal at the turn of the 20th century, Grand Central was then handling an estimated 13,600,000 passengers a year, and traffic managers saw no end to growth in traffic. It was largely because of the

This 1963 view shows the Grand Central concourse the way it looked when the station was still owned and operated by the New York Central. In 1968, New York Central merged with its archrival, the Pennsylvania Railroad. Today Grand Central Terminal is served by the Metro-North Commuter Railroad, which operates passenger services on former New York Central, and New Haven lines.

Richard Jay Solomon

enormous growth in suburban traffic, just three years after the 1899 remodeling, that New York Central decided an entirely new terminal was needed.

New York Central did not want to repeat the mistake of 1899 by providing merely a marginally larger station, but rather, it wanted to construct a terminal that would satisfy New York City's needs for decades to come. Such a terminal exceeded the bounds of traditional means. First of all, even in 1900, the sheer price of Manhattan real estate precluded acquiring the land required for a very large terminal in the center of the city. In addition to the space required for passenger facilities, a traditional design required acres for turning and servicing locomotives, coach yards, and an array of other crucial support services.

The locomotives themselves were an even more significant concern. Steam locomotives were dirty, sooty, smoky machines. With hundreds of trains a day rolling in and out of the terminal, the smoke problem had become unbearable, and even dangerous. The greatest concern was the approach to Grand Central through the Park Avenue tunnel, where smoke threatened to asphyxiate passengers, particularly during rush hours when trains paraded in and out of the station on short headways. Furthermore, smoke made it difficult for locomotive engineers to see lineside signals that controlled train movements and prevented rear-end collisions.

One proposed solution was the complete electrification of the railway into New York, a daunting, yet daring idea, despite the fact that it had never been tried on such a large scale before. The development of electrically powered street railways, and Baltimore & Ohio's short mainline electrification through new Baltimore tunnels, demonstrated the possibilities of railroad electrifica-

A daylight view of Grand Central's 42nd Street façade.

tion. As New York Central's officials pondered the potential of a new electrified terminal in the boardroom, events on the ground brought the question to a head. On the morning of January 8, 1902, a fully-loaded inbound New Haven commuter train paused in the Park Avenue and was struck from behind by another inbound train that overran a stop signal. When the dust settled, 15 people were dead. Although rear-end collisions were common in those days, this one precipitated a media frenzy which resulted in legislation forcing New York City's railways to electrify their lines. Suddenly, New York Central found that it needed to pioneer heavy mainline electric traction, and that the City of New York had established strict deadlines for its implementation.

The railroad set up an Electric Traction Commission, calling on many authorities in the field to assist in the planning of practical electrification. Work began in 1903, a prototype locomotive was built in 1904, and the first scheduled electric trains debuted in 1906. The New York Central developed a 660-volt, direct current system using an under-running third rail to power trains. (Trains received power from third rail shoes that collected current from the bottom side of the rail. The top was covered with a safety shield to minimize the chance of people or animals being accidentally electrocuted on the tracks.)

While electrification was underway, the plans for a new Grand Central were drawn up. Electrification permitted real estate-conserving bi-level construction, and allowed terminal tracks to be entirely covered over, thus permitting property development above the track. The use of electric traction greatly reduced the amount of space required for locomotive servicing, and greatly simplified operations. Electric multiple units used in suburban service were designed for bi-directional operation. So when a train arrived at the terminal, there was no locomotive that needed to be taken off the train, turned, and serviced. To reverse the multiple unit out of the station, the engineer simply had to change ends; even that was not necessary if the train arrived at a loop track.

The building architecture is the result of the dynamic synergy of two firms that were often at odds with one another over design details. Minnesota-based Reed & Stem, known for their railroad architecture, drew up the initial plans. The highly respected New York firm of Warren & Wetmore is credited for the refined elements of the design.

Whitney Warren had studied at the École des Beaux Arts in Paris, the school that greatly influenced the evolution of architecture in the late 19th and early 20th centuries. Students of the Beaux Arts designed many of America's most celebrated buildings. Earlier in his career, Warren had worked for McKim, Mead & White, who were later responsible for the design of New York's other great railway terminal, the much-celebrated Pennsylvania Station on 33rd Street.

After years of discussion, dissention, planning, and its eventual construction, the new Grand Central Terminal opened to the public in February 1913. Its monumental proportions, sublime style, and clever architectural plan were an immediate sensation. It was the latest shining jewel in New York's gilded crown, symbolizing the optimism and progressive attitude of the time. Grand Central was truly electrifying and it satisfied the need for a glamorous gateway to America's foremost metropolis. The public lauded its sumptuous detail and beauty, while intellectual iconoclasts dissected elements of its design.

New York City's other great passenger terminal was Pennsylvania Station. This beautiful building was one of the finest railway stations ever built and served the Pennsylvania Railroad, New Haven, and Long Island Rail Road for more than 50 years, until it was demolished between 1963 and 1965. The destruction of this wonderful station produced a public outcry that ultimately resulted in legislation to protect historic structures from corporate vandalism. Grand Central would have been destroyed, too, if it weren't for these laws.

Richard Jay Solomon

The immense statuary on Grand Central's 42nd street façade was the work of French sculptor Jules-Alexis Coutan. It depicts the mythical characters of Mercury (center), Hercules (left), and Minerva (right).

A hand-colored 1913 postcard view depicts Grand Central Terminal's 42nd Street façade when the station was new.

Richard Jay Solomon collection

Grand Central was finished in Bedford limestone and Stoney Creek granite. If one can delineate a "front" to this complex and multifaceted structure, it would have to be the magnificent 42nd Street façade where three arched windows, 60 feet tall and 33 feet wide, face south to take in the sun most of the day. Mimicking monumental porticos in classical architecture, these windows are bracketed by enormous Ionic pilasters. The exterior exhibits restrained ornamentation, and the minimal use of sculpture; however, an enormous statuary and giant, ornate clock—13 feet in diameter—sit above the central portico window. The statuary is the work of sculptor Jules Coutan who symbolically depicted the mythological figures of Mercury, Hercules, and Minerva. The great size and pomposity of the sculpture seemed out of place, and caused tirades of vitriolic criticism at the time. If by chance puzzled tourists fail to comprehend what stands before them, a giant plaque, carved in stone below the statue reads "Grand Central Terminal."

The interior lives up to expectation. The station's upper level concourse is an exercise in immensity. It is 275 feet long, 120 feet wide, and covered by a great parabolic ceiling rising 125 feet from the floor at its apex. This ceiling is decorated with an adaptation of the night sky, depicted (by error in its installation) in *reverse*, save for one significant constellation, which is portrayed in the normal way. The ceiling features an estimated 2,500 individual stars, the largest of which were lit originally with bulbs of varying brightness to mimic their actual luminosity in the night sky. (It is now lit with fiber optics to reduce bulb replacement maintenance.) This ceiling is one of the best ways to develop an appreciation for the heavens in New York City, where smog, skyscrapers, and city lights preclude a clear view of the evening sky. The Planetarium may provide a more spectacular rendition of the heavens, but you can't catch the express to New Haven from the Planetarium.

On one side of the concourse are entrances to upper-level platforms; on the opposite side are ticket counters. In the center of this vastness, stationed like an island on a serene stone lake, sits the information desk with its famous golden clock. Here, timetables are displayed, and one can get directions to sights all over the City, such as: "What track is the local to Poughkeepsie? Where can I find the Oyster Bar? Which subway takes me to Wall Street?" Directly below the Upper Level concourse is the suburban concourse providing access to the tracks on the Lower Level.

In the late 1990s, Grand Central received a massive renovation that restored much of its early glory to the station, and portions of the station that had been neglected since 1913 were finished. Although no longer serving long-distance trains, Grand Central remains a vital, active railroad terminal serving tens of thousands of commuters and a hundred thousand pedestrians and shoppers daily.

Current plans are underway to make the terminal even busier, as the Metropolitan Transportation Authority, now the owner of the structure, expects to build a third level of tracks below the arrival stations for the Long Island Rail Road to enter via the never-used lower level of the 63rd Street Tunnel from Queens. And, perhaps, some day, these tracks will be extended down Madison Avenue via a long-planned connection to Penn Station, making Grand Central truly the center of New York's extensive rail transit system.

Above: Enormous arched windows allow daylight to penetrate Grand Central's vast concourse. The station's ornate design is a wonderful contrast to the austere architecture of today.

Right: The ceiling of Grand Central's concourse is decorated with a reverse depiction of the night sky, complete with hundreds of lit stars.

The present-day Grand Central was made possible by the development of practical mainline railroad electrification. The entire Grand Central terminal trackage was electrified using an under-running third rail energized at 660 volts, direct current. In this February 2, 1958, photograph, New Haven Railroad FL9 2017 sits adjacent to a former Cleveland Union Terminal electric. The FL9 was a dual-mode (diesel-electric/electric) variant of the popular Electro-Motive F-unit that could operate from either the third rail or a 16-cylinder 567 engine.

Jim Shaughnessy

Leipzig Hauptbahnhof

A view from the concourse of the Leipzig Haupbahnhof to the platforms gives one a sense of the immensity of the station.

Rolling into the Leipzig Hauptbahnhof is like arriving by train at an immense arboretum, except you see trains in the place of trees. Unlike so many train sheds that have become vast, dark enclosures, shadowed by years of accumulated soot and grime, the Leipzig Hauptbahnhof, although vast, is bright and airy, thanks to a recent renovation. The station building is positively massive, and a testimony to the golden age of railway building.

Variously home to Bach, Wagner, and Goethe, Leipzig is an historic cultural center, and one of eastern Germany's largest cities. By the mid 19th century, Leipzig had developed into a major railway center, and was a choice location for trade fairs and conventions. Railway lines reached Leipzig from points all across the recently unified German kingdoms; Leipzig had no less than six major train stations. Unfortunately for the traveler, these stations were located at opposite ends of the city center, which complicated travel arrangements, especially when one needed to change trains. While many countries had tolerated these sorts of travel difficulties as railways expanded, accepting them as inevitable, Germans sought a better, more efficient, railway network. Leipzig was one of several major cities that saw a consolidation of its terminals in order to provide centrally located facilities. In 1907, work began on the new central Hauptbahnhof which was built to serve a variety of railway lines in the same fashion as the big American union stations, such as those in Washington, D.C., St. Louis, and Los Angeles.

The new Hauptbahnhof was located on the sight of the older Thüringer Bahnhöfe, just a few blocks' walk from the Sachsenplatz at the heart of the city center. In German, Hauptbahnhof means "main railway station," and is

The sheds at Leipzig Haupbahnhof were designed by Eilers & Karing, and designed to cover 26 tracks. Double-deck suburban passenger cars wait for passengers beneath the vast Leipzig sheds.

usually abbreviated Hbf. At the time of construction, the Hauptbahnhof was the source of great civic pride to the citizens of Leipzig, and the city absorbed about a third of the cost of construction. This was significant because the station was one of the most expensive ever built in Germany, and perhaps in Europe. By the time it was finally opened in 1915, at the start of World War I, it was by far the largest railway station in Europe.

The headhouse, designed by Dresden-based architects William Lossow and Max Hans Kühne, measured nearly 1,000 feet across and contained an immense passenger concourse 876 feet long. This gargantuan railway building with its monumental, three-tiered roof completely conceals the vast train sheds that rest behind it. The sheds are the work of engineers Eilers & Karing, and consist of six spans. Each span is 147 feet wide and almost 900 feet long, originally covering 26 tracks and 13 broad platforms. A massive transept, 80 feet wide, bridges the six longitudinal spans with the headhouse. According to John A. Droege, in his 1916 book, *Passenger Terminals and Trains*, the entire station occupied 882,642 square feet. To support the station, more than 3,000 reinforced concrete piles were driven into the ground.

The Leipzig Hbf was born in a world of strife, and its heyday was clouded by war and chaos. During World War II, Leipzig was pounded by Allied bombs. Following the war, Leipzig was in the territory under the control of the Soviet-satellite Deutsche Demokratische Republik (German Democratic Republic), commonly described in the West as "East Germany." Under the Soviet-style socialist economy, the Hauptbahnhof suffered from neglect and became a ghastly, cavernous shadow of its former glory. Ironically, this condition was not

Leipzig Hbf was beautifully renovated in the 1990s and now also contains a large shopping plaza on the lower levels.

unlike that suffered by many of the once-grand railway terminals in the United States for different reasons. While economists and political scientists can argue the differences between the two economic regimes, to the casual observer, the fate of the Leipzig Hauptbahnhof seemed similar to that of stations in America.

Fortunately for Leipzig, the tide turned and, following the reunification of Germany in 1990, the Hauptbahnhof was renovated and its great shed restored. In 2002, Leipzig Hbf is again a vital, beautiful station. A few of the tracks beneath the shed on the south side of the station have been removed to make way for an automobile parking garage. As a tribute to the wonders and excesses of the Capitalist economy, the station headhouse has been modified to contain a massive three-story shopping center built on the American model. Once immersed in the bright lights and glitz of the shops, a traveler is blissfully unaware of the trains rolling in out of the station shed above.

Leipzig Hbf is served by a network of electric trams that help disperse passengers to all corners of the city, and many passengers may find that their destinations are within a short walk of the station. A great number of trains roll in and out of Leipzig daily, and there are through services to many cities across Germany, including Berlin, Dresden, München (Munich), Frankfurt, and Köln (Cologne). In addition to regional and intercity trains, Leipzig Hbf is now served by some of Germany's finest and fastest trains, the acclaimed high-speed InterCity Expresses, or ICE trains. While Leipzig doesn't sit on a high-speed route, these trains reach the station over conventional lines and offer a higher quality of service than ever before.

A detailed view of the steel work that comprises the sheds at the Leipzig Hauptbahnhof.

Helsinki Station

A morning view of the Helsinki Station as it appears in the city center. Some art historians consider the Helsinki Station as the division point in Finnish architecture. Later buildings abandoned the strong nationalistic elements and followed more international trends.

Conveniently located in the heart of central Helsinki is VR's (Finnish State Railways) main railway station. This striking structure is one of the world's great railway terminal buildings, and one of only a few that embodies an art nouveau aesthetic. Helsinki Station was constructed between 1911 and 1914, toward the end of the great station building period in Europe. It has less in common with traditional railway terminals, instead sharing similarities with other civil buildings in Helsinki or elsewhere in Finland. Traditional railway stations typically used variations of neo-classical or neo-gothic architecture, as typified by Washington Union Station (pages 72 to 73) and London's St. Pancras (pages 68 to 71) respectively.

The history of Finnish Railways is integral to the cultural and political history between Finland and Russia. Most of the railway lines in Finland were built during the period of Czarist Russian domination, and as a result, Finland uses the Russian five-foot track gauge (rather than the standard 4 feet 8.5 inches used in most of non-Russian Europe). Interestingly, the Russian gauge was established by George Washington Whistler (see pages 97 to 99), an American who built Russia's first railway in the 1840s.

Helsinki station was the work of one of Finland's greatest and best-known architects, Eliel Saarinen. Inspired by the Vienna Secession movement, Saarinen designed using a blend of elements of the Arts & Crafts movement with themes from traditional Finnish rural architecture to produced decidedly romantic and nationalistic styles. At the time he was working, in the early 20th century, Finland was enjoying a reactionary nationalistic movement in the arts following a period of cultural oppression between 1899-1905 when Czarist influences had tried unsuccessfully to "Russify" Fin-

The clock tower is a traditional element found in railway station designs around the world. Helsinki Station features an enormous granite clock tower, 159 feet tall, on the eastern side of the station.

land. Saarinen's nationalistic architecture is equivalent to the music of Jean Sibelius, whose works, such as *Finlandia*, reflect strong Finnish patriotism. Finland was freed from Russian domination in 1917 on the eve of the Soviet Era. The Helsinki station was finally dedicated in 1919, roughly five years after it was completed.

The layout of Helsinki Station is a typical stub terminal with a headhouse building. Because of Helsinki's geographic position on a peninsula, and its political significance as both the capital and largest city in Finland, there is no need for a "through" station, as virtually all passenger trains terminate here. Saarinen's station replaced an earlier facility that dated to 1861. The style of the new station is characterized by simplicity and visual massiveness, common features of Finnish art nouveau designs. The frontal façade features a great portal archway flanked by pairs of giant, masculine statues holding large globes. The outer walls are constructed of typical Finnish granite, while the interior vaults are made from reinforced concrete—a relatively new construction material at the time. (One of the premises of art nouveau was the employment of new materials such as steel and concrete in place of more conventional materials.) The station and tracks are at ground level, and three principal entrances allow passengers easy access to trains and booking facilities. An enormous granite clock tower is situated near the eastern entrance. The tower is 48.5 meters (159 feet) tall and features giant clock faces 3.3 meters (10.8 feet) in diameter.

Over the years there have been many alterations to Helsinki Station; some were planned, others were not. A central hall nearer the tracks than the main hall was built in 1925. In 1944, a bombing raid substantially damaged the roof of the administration wing, which was subsequently rebuilt, albeit in a slightly different style. A fire in 1950 again damaged part of the station, which needed to be rebuilt. Traditionally, there was no shed over the tracks, which left them exposed to the elements and, as one might expect, this was uncomfortable for passengers, particularly in the harsh Finnish winter. Recently this was rectified, and a modern cantilever shed now protects the main tracks, nearest the main terminal, that are used for long-distance express trains. The tracks are electrified at 25 kV alternating current at 50 Hz, and all trains are electrically powered.

Today, Helsinki station is a busy terminal accommodating about 400 passenger trains a day in each direction. The majority are suburban passenger trains, while there are about 60 pairs of long-distance trains a day. Through international service jointly run with the Russian railways travel is available to St. Petersburg and Moscow. Suburban traffic is on the rise: in 2001, roughly 71,000 people used the station daily. Commuter traffic has been growing at a rate of 2-3 percent per year, while long-distance traffic has declined slightly in recent years. Presently the station has 19 tracks and is near capacity.

Saarinen also designed a similar railway station that was located at Viipuri (Vyborg); this beautiful building was damaged during World War II. Viipuri, once part of Finland, is now in Russia as result of a border change following the War. Eliel Saarinen migrated to the United States in 1923, and both he and his son, Eero Saarinen, made important architectural contributions in America.

This interior view of Helsinki Station displays the station's eclectic, minimalist architectural style. Compare this station with New York's Grand Central Terminal, which was built around the same time. Helsinki is an example of art nouveau, while Grand Central is beaux-arts.

Here is a detailed view of the arch on Helsinki Station's southern entrance. Weekdays, 71,000 commuters and 15,000 long-distance passengers use the station that is conveniently situated in the Helsinki city center.

A Finnish State Railways express train arrives at Helsinki in August 2001. VR's 3000 Class electrics were built by the Soviet Union in the 1970s. Finland still uses the Russian broad gauge—five feet between the rails.

A detailed view of the larger-than-life statues that grace the southern façade of Saarinen's Helsinki Station.

Milano Centrale

Milano Centrale was built on a superhuman scale. Its massive proportions, blockish, stone architecture, and classical symbolism embodied elements of the Fascist Ideal despite the fact the station had been designed in the World War I period.

The monumental façade of Milano Stazione Centrale (Milan Central Station) faces a great open plaza near the heart of the city. This immense building is the headhouse to one of the last great railway stations built in Europe.

Milan is a large industrial center and a strategic international terminal in northern Italy. In its search for a new central railway terminal in the second decade of the 20th century, Milan held an architectural competition to procure a suitable design. Ulisse Stacchini won the competition in 1913. This was a late start for such a significant terminal. Many American and European cities had already completed large stations by the time Milan entered the planning stage. New York's Grand Central Terminal was completed in 1913, and two years later, the last of the great German terminals, the Leipzig Haupbahnhof (see pages 82 to 83) was finished.

The Milan station faced repeated construction delays; World War I and the financial distress that followed the war set back construction by more than a decade. Work finally began in 1925, and six years later the station was completed.

The station headhouse is fronted by an enormous colonnade 607 feet long, 90 feet high, and 79 feet wide that provides a vestibule covering a roadway used by vehicular traffic serving the station. The colonnade features three huge porticos each of which is 29.5 feet wide and 53 feet high. The booking hall (where passengers purchase their tickets) is of similarly huge proportions, and decorated with Roia marble and travertine stone. Connecting the booking hall and the concourse are great stairways to reach the tracks, located some 25 feet above street level. The elevated platforms permit several important streets to pass below the station. The main concourse, located at track level, measures 705 feet long, 72 feet wide, and 82 feet high. Today, the concourse also serves as a shopping arcade and offers several restaurants. Huge skylights filter light into the concourse, counteracting the inherent gloom from its tremendous, vault-like verticality.

The massive terminal building is accompanied by a shed, covering the platform area, of equivalent proportions. Milan's sheds are an architectural anomaly, completed a generation after others in Europe. These five great steel arches were the last traditional balloon-type sheds to be built. The arched shed was introduced in 1867 at St. Pancras, London (see page 68), and remained popular through the early years of the last century. By the advent of World War I, the arched design had fallen out of style in favor of "Butterfly canopies" and other methods of sheltering passengers. By the time Milan's shed was built, similar arches in America were being dismantled. Milan Central's platforms were built to a length of 1,051 feet. The central shed is the largest of the five, measuring 110 feet tall with a span of 236 feet. Bracketing it are two smaller sheds, each 72 feet, 3 inches tall, spanning 147 feet; the outermost sheds are smaller yet again, measuring just 37 feet 9 inches tall, with spans of 69 feet at the open end.

Milan Central's grandiose style and superhuman scale has generated both admiration and criticism. It had been heralded as one of the "Railway Wonders of the World" in a 1935 book of that name. But Carroll Meeks also lambasted it in his definitive book, *The Railroad Station*, as being "bombastic, and retrogressively monumental." In their book, *The Railway Station; A Social History*, authors Jeffery Richards and John M. MacKenzie explain that Milan Central's monumental size, gigantic proportions, and blockish, bold architecture, fulfilled ideals set forth by the Fascist movement that drove Italy during the 1930s, despite the fact the design and construction predated the Fascist period.

The gargantuan balloon train sheds at Milano Centrale dwarf the trains below them.

Milano Centrale has five balloon sheds, of which the center shed is by far the largest. It is seen in February 2000, covering Italy's fastest train, the ETR 500.

The station's enormous arched train sheds were the largest, and the last, ever built. By the time these balloon sheds were constructed, the style had completely fallen out of fashion in the rest of the world.

Section Three

RAILWAY ENGINEERING

Furka-Oberalp Bahn's branch from Andermatt to Götschenen descends a fantastic 17.9 percent grade through a series of tunnels and snowsheds, making it one of the most interesting short train rides in the world. In February 2000, an F-O train approaches Götschenen near the north portal of SBB's famous St. Gotthard Tunnel.

The First Mountain Railroad

A westbound Conrail freight ascends the east slope of Washington Hill, crossing a vintage stone arch bridge over the West Branch of the Westfield River a few miles from Chester, Massachusetts.

In the forest, on the east slope of the Berkshires in Western Massachusetts, stand stone arch bridges dating from the earliest days of the railway. The arches seem positively ancient, as if built by long-ago civilizations for a purpose now unknown. In a sense, they *are* ancient, as their design has its roots in Roman architecture, which found its way to America via Britain's industrial revolution.

The formative years of American transportation engineering was dominated by east-west schemes designed to connect the developing interior of the country with major East Coast ports. Prosperous states were eager to secure their share of lucrative interior traffic. New York had acted first with the construction of the Erie Canal, which directed traffic through New York City. Maryland encouraged the construction of the Baltimore & Ohio Railroad (see Grasshoppers, pages 11 to 12), and Pennsylvania pushed forward its Main Line of Public Works (see The Horseshoe Curve, page 106). New England saw its fortunes were seriously hampered with the advent of the Erie Canal. By virtue of geography, New England ports faced greater distances from the developing interior markets than New York, Philadelphia, or Baltimore. New England's most important port, Boston, hoped to overcome geographical impediments by the construction of a railway over the Berkshires to Albany, New York. Such a proposal seemed absurd to the conventional wisdom of the day, yet its construction commenced, anyway.

By 1833, the Boston & Worcester had connected its namesake cities. The Western Railroad (often described as the Western Railroad of Massachusetts) was chartered to reach from the end of the B&W across Massachusetts to the New York state line, where it was to connect

Above: A detailed view, showing the stonework on one of Whistler's stone arch bridges near milepost 129, east of Middlefield, Massachusetts.

Below: The largest remaining Whistler stone arch bridge is located near milepost 130 about one half mile from the old Middlefield Station. This bridge has not been used since 1912 when New York Central built a short line relocation to ease the curvature on the east slope of the Berkshires.

with lines to the Hudson River. Major George Washington Whistler, one of the foremost railway engineers of his day, was the line's chief engineer. Whistler had learned railroading working for the B&O, and was among those who traveled to Britain to study early railway practices (see the section on Grasshoppers). Later, he worked on the construction and operation of several New England lines.

Whistler surveyed and built the Western over terrain more difficult than had yet been conquered by any other railway in the world. Although the Berkshires are relatively tame in comparison with other mountain ranges, they were considered wild and rugged in the 1830s, and presented a formidable barrier to the West. Whistler surveyed his route in 1836, and tracks had reached the Connecticut River at Springfield by 1839. The Western faced a fairly steep climb immediately after leaving Worcester bringing the line over Charlton Summit, but the most difficult section of the railroad to build and to operate was the eastern ascent of the Berkshires. Whistler was convinced he could tackle this section using an adhesion grade, rather than an inclined plane, despite the fact that no railroad had yet been built using prolonged adhesion grades. Many railway builders didn't understand friction, mistakenly believing that steam locomotives with iron wheels on iron tracks would be incapable of ascending graded track. Early locomotives such as Robert Stephenson's *Rocket* (see page 9) had only recently demonstrated a locomotive's ability to climb a slight grade, and no operator had yet attempted a line like Whistler's.

He wasn't content with a shoddily constructed line and insisted on the best possible grade by using cuts, fills, stone retaining walls, and large stone arch bridges. Although only a single track was needed in the first years of the railroad, Whistler had the insight to grade as much

Whistler's arched bridges date from the construction of the railroad in the late 1830s and early 1840s. Compare the unfinished stonework of this bridge, located near Middlefield, Massachusetts, with the more refined brick design of the Ouse Valley Viaduct (pictured on page 102) built at the same time in Britain. This bridge is one of three that was abandoned in 1912, yet remains standing more than 90 years later.

line as possible for the eventuality of double track. His vision produced remarkably good engineering for the period, but his policy of building a high quality line got him in difficulty with the railroad's directors. By the time the Western was opened to through traffic in 1842, it was the longest stretch of railroad ever constructed under the direction of one company and, according to Alvin F. Harlow's *Steelways of New England*, it was also the most expensive. Whistler didn't stay with the Western very long and went on to build Russia's first railway, connecting Moscow with St. Petersburg. His Western line had set an important precedent in the United States, though, and his line was so well engineered that 160 years after it was finished the majority of his original alignment is still in use as a main line.

The most remarkable part of Whistler's Berkshire crossing is the steepest section between Chester and Washington Summit. Here, the railroad closely follows the west branch of the Westfield River (which it crosses repeatedly in just a few miles), and the gradient reaches a maximum of 1.67 percent. Between milepost 128—measured from Boston—and milepost 131, Whistler crossed the river and its tributaries seven times, and designed a series of rugged stone arch bridges, similar to those used by the B&O. It is clear that Whistler had taken his inspiration from the early British lines that preferred this type of construction.

According to the publication *Stone Walls*, a booklet about The Western Rail-road published in Huntington, Massachusetts, the bridges were built by a Scottish stonemason named Alexander Birnie, who used teams of Irish, Italian, and Russian immigrants to cut and fit the stones. While the arches were under construction, wooden frames were erected to support the stones, many of which weighed 500 lbs. Once the arches were completed, the frames were removed and the weight of the bridge made it self-supporting. Today, five stone bridges still stand, although only two still carry tracks. About a mile of Whistler's 1841 alignment was abandoned in 1912 when the difficult section between mileposts 129 and 130 was rebuilt to ease the curvature and make room for a third track. On this short stretch of disused line just below the old Middlefield Station (on some maps, near the village of Bancroft) is the location of three of Whistler's arches. A sixth stone arch bridge of similar construction is still in use on the east end of the line across the Quaboag River near West Warren, Massachusetts.

In 1867, the Western merged with the Boston & Worcester to form the Boston & Albany. This company was leased to the New York Central in 1900, but retained considerable independence as part of the New York Central system. Locomotives and equipment were lettered for the B&A until the 1950s, and many railroaders still know the line as "the B&A" despite the formal dissolution of the company in the 1960s, and subsequent changes in ownership of the line. The route that Whistler laid out in the 1830s is still very much alive. In 1999, CSX assumed freight operation of the old Boston & Albany line from Conrail and now operates between 15 and 20 freights daily over the route. Amtrak provides service through the Berkshire's with its daily *Lake Shore Limited* that connects Boston and Chicago.

In August 1989, a General Electric C32-8 leads a Conrail intermodal train through the deep cut at Washington, Massachusetts on the east slope of the Berkshires. This line was surveyed by Major George W. Whistler in the 1830s and still serves as a primary freight corridor. The cutting was made the hard way, with charges of black powder, axes, and shovels. The bridge over the top of the cut was originally the turntable at West Springfield.

Several stone arch bridges on the old Western Railroad remain in daily service. The line is now operated by CSX and serves as a primary rail-freight corridor to New England from the West. An eastbound CSX auto-rack train crosses a double stone arch over the Quaboag River at West Warren, Massachusetts, in October 2000.

Ouse Valley Viaduct

On a July 2001 evening, a suburban passenger train rumbles across the Ouse Valley Viaduct. This elegant viaduct is located a few miles north of Hayward Heath in Sussex.

Spanning the Ouse Valley in central Sussex, (south of England) is a stunning brick and stone viaduct that carries the old Brighton Line, a railway connecting its namesake with London. Although the River Ouse is not one of the great rivers in Britain—it is in fact, little more than a country stream—over the aeons its meandering course has cut a relatively deep and broad valley that presented a difficult obstacle to early railway engineers. British railways were engineered to very high standards; the lines were built as straight and as level as possible within the bounds of practicality. Economy-minded railway builders might have engineered lines that closely followed the contours of the land, resulting in longer, steeper, and more sinuous routes. Such a line would be cheaper to build, but more expensive to operate. The Brighton Line was surveyed by Sir John Rennie, one of Britain's most acclaimed early railway engineers, and the viaduct itself was designed by John U. Rastrick. It was constructed in 1841.

A viaduct is a bridge comprised of a series of short spans. The Ouse Valley Viaduct has 37 arches and is 1475 feet long. Each arch spans 30 feet, and the bridge is 96 feet tall at its highest point over the valley. What is especially unusual about this viaduct is not its height or length, but the distinctive design of its arches. Instead of making each support solid, which was common in contemporary stone bridge design, a large oval-like section was left open in each of the supports in order to keep the weight of the bridge to a minimum and, presumably, to strengthen it as well.

Looking down the length of the viaduct from below results in a remarkable view through the seemingly concentric oval spaces, resembling the view to infinity created by placing two mirrors opposite one another. This quality, combined with

Each arch of the Ouse Valley Viaduct has large, oval openings. The openings were created to reduce the weight and the cost of the bridge. By standing at either end below the viaduct, and looking down the length of the bridge through the openings, you can get this unique perspective.

other refined, aesthetic elements of its design, such as the Gothic towers at either end of the bridge, have led architectural historians to proclaim the Ouse Valley Viaduct as one of the most handsome in Britain. The railings that run along the top of the bridge mimic the overall viaduct in miniature when viewed in profile.

The viaduct is no less impressive now than it was 160 years ago. It stands as a stark silhouette in an otherwise pastoral setting. The immense bridge seems incongruous with the low, lightly rolling hills, small copse of trees, and winding country lanes that characterize the surrounding countryside. Without warning, it seems to rise out of nowhere, cut across the horizon, and vanish again. Motorists driving past it on a nearby road will slow in awe to take in its size and beauty. While now viewed as an architectural remnant of an earlier age and a symbol of the steam era, it was once seen as *modern* … the very symbol of man's progress.

Over the years, tens of thousands of trains have crossed the two-track viaduct. The Brighton Line, once the route of such famous trains as the *Brighton Belle*, brought passengers in style from inner-city London to seaside resorts at its namesake. The line became part of the Southern Railway during the grouping of 1923 (which assembled four large regional railway systems out of the myriad of lines in Great Britain). It was also one of the earliest routes to be electrified on what would eventually become the world's most extensive, third-rail-electrified, suburban passenger network. Today electrified passenger trains still roll across the Ouse Valley as they have for generations; all day long, every few minutes, a train bound to or from London will clatter across the bridge. Its longevity is a testimony to its designers, and a fine example of the high quality of workmanship that exemplified early British railway engineering.

The railings running along the top of the Ouse Valley Viaduct mimic the structure of the bridge in miniature. This especially elegant viaduct is among the oldest, large railway bridges in the world still in regular daily use. It was built in 1841, the same time as Whistler's arches in the Berkshires of Massachusetts.

The clear, summer sun illuminates the 160-year old Ouse Valley Viaduct. Notice the oval holes in each of the support piers.

The Horseshoe Curve

The combination of bucolic splendor, heavy traffic, and engineering mastery has helped make Pennsylvania's Horseshoe Curve one of America's foremost train-watching spots. A long Conrail intermodal train winds its way past Kittanning Point as it works westward around Horseshoe Curve on July 30, 1987. A two-unit helper shoves at the back of the train.

A horseshoe curve is a track arrangement that, seen on a map or viewed from above, resembles the shape of a common horseshoe. Many railway lines have used sweeping horseshoe curves to gain elevation, and they are relatively common on lines in the western United States.

Horseshoe curves, like other significant sections of railway line such as bridges and tunnels, often carry names. For example the Leonard Horseshoe is on the Union Pacific main line through Oregon's Blue Mountains. This relatively obscure horseshoe curve is located between Durkee and Oxman, a few miles from Encina Summit. Deep in Cold Stream Canyon, west of Truckee, California, on the east slope of the old Central Pacific Donner Pass crossing, is Stanford Curve, named for Leland Stanford, a former California governor, and one of the "Big Four" who financed and built the railroad.

There are many more truly obscure horseshoes laid out in the rocks and sagebrush of the American West. But when one mentions *The* Horseshoe curve, no clarification is required: The Horseshoe Curve, in a bucolic Appalachian valley just west of Altoona, Pennsylvania, on the former Pennsylvania Railroad main line, is the most spectacular, and certainly the most famous of all railroad horseshoes.

Horseshoe Curve was built in 1854, as the PRR was pushing its line westward to connect Philadelphia and Pittsburgh with an all-rail route. This new route replaced the curious, but tedious and cumbersome, Main Line of Public Works, a railroad-canal-portage railway route. Heralded as a gift of modern transportation when it opened in 1834, the Main Line of Public Works provided much faster transportation through the mountains than the crude roads and

Above: The public park at the center of Horseshoe Curve is designed for casual train watchers. In November 2001, people gather to see Amtrak's *Pennsylvanian* climbing westward around the curve. The train is led by two GE GENESIS diesels, a type that has become Amtrak's standard diesel power.

Below: This wide-angle postcard view of the Horseshoe Curve distorts the perspective of the tracks in the foreground, but allows for a clearer understanding of the relationship between the curve and the surrounding landscape. Looking east, the tracks on the left are descending toward Altoona while those on the right are climbing toward the summit of the Alleghenies at Gallitzin.

footpaths across Pennsylvania that preceded it. Travel time from Philadelphia to Pittsburgh over this route was four-and-a-half days. The most interesting aspect of the Main Line of Public Works, and its ultimate undoing, was its portage railway section between Holidaysburg and Johnstown, where 10 inclined planes were used to hoist canal packet boats up and over the mountains. An inclined plane was a short, but exceptionally steep section (using 8- to 10-percent grades in the case of the Main Line) of railroad that was operated by a system of cables powered by a stationary steam engine rather than a steam locomotive. While inclined planes were by no means unique to the Main Line (they were used by many early railways), the Main Line's extensive use of a portage railway network to haul canal boats over the Allegheny Divide has no parallel in American transport. (At the Allegheny Divide, also known as the Eastern Continental Divide, water flowing east ends up in the Atlantic, while water flowing west ends up in the Gulf of Mexico.)

The Pennsylvania Railroad route across the mountains was laid out by J. Edgar Thomson. This visionary engineer was one of the best-qualified railroad men of his day. He was the son of a surveyor, and had spent fifteen years building and operating railways before coming to the Pennsylvania Railroad. Early in his career, Thomson had worked on both the Camden & Amboy and Philadelphia & Columbia, two companies that would later become integral parts of the PRR system. Like other early American railway engineers, Thomson had traveled to Britain to study railway practices there. His multifaceted railroad experience gave him the insight to design a railroad with ease of operations in mind, a talent that clearly paid off. As the railroad was building westward, he assumed the presidency of the line. Under his leadership, the Pennsylvania Railroad eventually became one of the most important American railways, and one of the most powerful companies in the country.

Thomson's operational experience taught him that it would be cheaper to operate one relatively short, but steeply graded section over the mountains, rather than work with a prolonged, but moderately graded line. So, running west from Harrisburg, Thomson laid out a low-grade route along the Susquehanna and Juniata rivers as far as present-day Altoona. This is where the line must ascend the Allegheny Divide, the same ridge the Main Line crossed with the Portage Railway. The easy grade ends abruptly, and the stiff climbing begins. At Alto Tower in Altoona, the gradient change is clearly visible to the naked eye: the grade increases from 0.36 percent to 1.57 percent. Within a few miles, it reaches the maximum westbound grade of 1.85 percent. To maintain a constant climb and keep the gradient within reasonable limits, Thomson laid out the great sweeping Horseshoe, which begins along the north side of a valley near Kittaning Point (southwest of Altoona) and straightens back out again on the south side, so gaining 72 feet as result of the detour. In just under 10 miles, the railroad climbs 846 feet and crests in tunnels below the Allegheny Divide at Gallitzin. Beyond Gallitzin, the railroad descends toward Johnstown on a less severe gradient. Between Johnstown and Pittsburgh the railroad crosses a series of short summits that pose less of an operational difficulty than the big climb to Gallitzin.

There are numerous spectacular mountain railroads in the United States, and while many of these feature more

Above: Getting freight over the Alleghenies has always been a struggle. On April 3, 1988, a pair of Conrail SD45-2s working as Altoona-based helpers shove a westbound past Kittanning point and around Horseshoe Curve. These 20-cylinder monsters were built for Erie Lackawanna but spent much of their careers as Horseshoe Curve helpers.

Below: A westbound Conrail piggyback train exits the summit tunnel at Gallitzin, Pennsylvania in the summer of 1989.

difficult line profiles with stiffer grades and sharper curves than the PRR's Allegheny crossing, no mountain line carried more traffic than the mighty Pennsylvania Railroad main line. This line over the mountain around the Horseshoe Curve was built for two tracks, and by the end of 1854, both tracks were operational. By 1900, the line had been expanded to four main tracks to accommodate the increasing flow of traffic. At its peak, more than 100 freight and passenger trains traversed the Horseshoe Curve on an average day. As late as the early 1950s, the Pennsylvania Railroad operated more than 40 scheduled passenger movements over the line, and sometimes heavy passenger trains operated in two or more sections (see the *Twentieth Century Limited*, pages 18 to 21, for an explanation of "sections"). With a full complement of mixed-freight, coal, and ore trains running over the line, the PRR made excellent use of its four-track railroad, and it wasn't uncommon to see all four tracks around the Horseshoe curve occupied simultaneously.

The decline in passenger traffic from the late 1950s to the early 1970s, combined with changes in freight railroad operations, lessened the need for a four-track line through the mountains. The Pennsylvania Railroad merged with its long-time rival, New York Central, in 1968, forming Penn Central. A few years later, this enormous company floundered into the largest bankruptcy the world had yet seen. In 1976, the Federal Government created Conrail to assume operations on Penn Central and other bankrupt Northeastern railroads. During the early Conrail era, there was an emphasis on eliminating unnecessary trackage and trimming the physical plant to a more manageable size. Many lines that were deemed unprofitable, redundant, or otherwise unnecessary were sold or abandoned. In 1981, Conrail lifted the old No. 2 track around the Horseshoe Curve, and converted the No. 3 track to bi-directional operation. Despite this track reduction, the railroad has remained extremely busy. Under Conrail, freight traffic swelled and by the mid 1980s, 50 to 60 heavy freights a day were traversing the Horseshoe Curve. Not only were more

freight trains operating over the line than in earlier years, but also these trains had grown much longer and heavier. Clearance improvements in the mid 1990s allowed the operation of double stack intermodal trains, thereby adding several big trains a day to the line. In 1999, Conrail was divided between Norfolk Southern and CSX, and today NS runs the old PRR main line. Freight traffic remains robust and, in addition,

there are two daily Amtrak trains in each direction over the Curve.

The combination of scenic splendor, skilled engineering, and exceptionally heavy traffic has made the Horseshoe Curve a legend in the annals of railroading. The Curve was landscaped in 1879, and was often featured on old postcards and in Pennsylvania Railroad company literature. In 1940, a visitors' park opened at the center of the Curve

to give the public a safe vantage point from which to watch the daily parade of trains over the mountain. In the early 1990s the visitors' center was improved and remodeled, complete with a short funicular railway to bring people to track level. The Horseshoe Curve has long been famous, and remains today one of the most popular places in the United States to experience heavy railroading in action.

A Conrail freight rounds Horseshoe Curve westbound in the summer of 1988. For many years, one of the Pennsylvania Railroad K-4s Pacifics was displayed at Horseshoe Curve. In the 1980s, the steam locomotive was exchanged for an Electro-Motive GP9 diesel electric, which is seen to the right of this photo.

Pennsylvania's Great Viaducts
Starrucca Viaduct

The majesty of Starrucca is best appreciated from a distance. An eastbound Conrail freight rolls across Starrucca in the fading light of March 7, 1988.

The New York and Erie Railroad was conceived to connect the lower Hudson Valley at Piermont, New York with Lake Erie at Dunkirk, New York. The railroad was to remain within the state of New York as it was intended for the benefit of that state's citizens. Despite this intention, geography dictated that the line would cross into Pennsylvania, a matter that caused considerable controversy at the time.

Unlike other early American railways, which had adopted the Stephenson Standard gauge (4 feet 8.5 inches), Erie's engineers selected a broad gauge of six feet. This move was in part inspired by Isambard Kingdom Brunel's Great Western Railway in Britain, which used a 7 foot-1/4 inch gauge. In addition to offering greater stability, a broad gauge allowed for the use of much larger (and presumably more powerful) locomotives, and larger freight and passenger cars. The Erie was the broadest gauge commercial railroad in North America, although several other lines, including Atlantic & St. Lawrence, and Louisville & Nashville also used broad gauge tracks. Until the 1880s, many lines in the American Southeast used 5-foot gauge tracks.

The Erie followed the Delaware River west of Port Jervis, and enjoyed a water-level profile until it reached Deposit, New York. Here it faced more difficult terrain to climb over Gulf Summit, to Susquehanna, Pennsylvania, where the line again followed a relatively level alignment, along the Susquehanna River to Binghamton, New York. Erie's Gulf Summit crossing gave its engineers some of their greatest challenges. At the summit, the line runs through a deep rock cutting, then dips into Pennsylvania for a second time west of Port Jervis. Beyond the state line, the railroad crosses the valley of Starrucca Creek at Lanesboro. It is here that Erie's engineers built the magnificent stone bridge known as Starrucca Viaduct.

Railroad engineering was still a closely-knit trade in those times. Early engineers not only knew and worked with each other, but several were related. Julius Walker Adams and his Scottish-born brother-in-law, James Pugh Kirkwood, were Erie's engineers. Adams was also George W. Whistler's nephew and, like Whistler and other early American railway engineers, Adams was a West Point graduate. It is no coincidence that both Adams and Kirkword worked on the building of Whistler's Western in the Berkshires of Massachusetts, including the construction of Whistler's stone arched bridges on that line's east slope (see page 97).

Neither is it a coincidence that the Western and Erie were built using similar construction techniques, a fact that is still evident today. It seems logical that Adams and Kirkwood chose a similar—although grander—stone arched bridge construction for the Erie's Starrucca Viaduct, as used by Whistler on the Western. However, as William D. Middleton points out in his excellent book, *Landmarks on the Iron Road*, stone arch bridge construction had largely fallen out of favor by the mid-1840s because of its high cost. Not only was Starrucca the last of the great stone bridges from the formative period of American railroad building, but it was the single most expensive bridge built in America at that time. Erie's other large bridges, including the great Cascade Bridge near Gulf Summit, and the huge Portage Viaduct across the Genesee River, were originally constructed of wood. William S. Young points out that neither of these sites would have been good sites for stone bridges. Stone bridges would eventually come back in fashion, but not until a generation after Starrucca was completed.

The Erie needed to reach Binghamton by the end of 1848 in order to fulfill its charter, so Adams and Kirkwood had to erect Starrucca Viaduct quickly and efficiently. Kirkwood directed a team of 800 men, and built 17 solid, but graceful, arches across the valley. Starrucca is made from quarried sandstone known as "Bluestone." Each arch is 50 feet wide, and the highest of them rise 110 feet above the valley floor. It is 1,040 feet long and 26 feet wide. Because of the parapets, upon which tracks couldn't be laid, the bridge wasn't wide enough for two six-foot gauge tracks (although in broad gauge days a gauntlet arrangement was used over the bridge whereby the two tracks overlapped, permitting just one train at a time over the bridge).

Starrucca was completed on November 23, 1848, and the first locomotive rolled across it a couple of weeks later on December 9th. This was a significant test, because in those days, bridge design was more of an empirical art. Bridge failures were an all-too-common occurrence. Starrucca withstood the test, and not only was it fully capable of supporting the trains of the period, but it has proved strong enough to withstand the much heavier trains of today. With Starrucca completed, track laying proceeded more or less according to schedule, and the Erie met its deadline—the first train rolled into Binghamton a few days before New Year's Eve 1848.

When the Erie reached Dunkirk (its first western terminus) in 1851, it was the longest railroad in the United States operated by one company. Over the years it gradually extended lines to other cities and eventually reached Chicago. In its heyday, the Erie was the smallest of the four great Eastern trunk lines (the others being the Baltimore & Ohio, New York Central, and Pennsylvania Railroads) that connected the East Coast with the Midwest. In its day, Erie moved a considerable volume of freight over Starrucca.

The west slope of Gulf Summit features a 1.2 percent grade, which presented a significant operating challenge for eastbound trains. Heavier-than-necessary locomotives were often assigned to freights climbing the grade for the more level parts of the railroad to the west, and helpers were often used to shove trains up the grade to Gulf Summit. For this reason, the Erie selected a site located a few miles east of Starrucca near the base of the grade as a division point where locomotives and crews were exchanged. This grew into the village of Susquehanna, which owes its existence to the Erie. Here the railroad built locomotive shops, servicing facilities and yards, as well as its famous Starrucca House hotel, restaurant, and station. In the days before dining cars, Erie's passenger trains would pause here while passengers dined at the station's large neo-gothic dining hall. These facilities were an important part of Erie's operations. Most were closed following the Erie-Lackawanna merger of 1960, after which the former Erie line over Starrucca gradually lost its importance.

Although the line east of Binghamton is still maintained as a through route, in modern times little traffic has been routed this way. Under Conrail in the mid to late 1980s, the old Erie saw a mild resurgence of traffic when it was for a short time the preferred route for double-stack container traffic. The Erie's broad gauge route, converted to standard gauge in the 1880s, had ample clearances to accommodate the taller cars—a boon other routes in the region

did not have until they were substantially rebuilt. New York,
Susquehanna & Western acquired
haulage rights over the Erie line to
Binghamton in the mid-1980s, and
has used this route for its double-
stack trains and other traffic. Conrail eventually improved the clearances on both the former New York
Central "Water Level Route" and
the old Pennsylvania Railroad
mainline (via Horseshoe Curve, see
page 106).

Since 1999, the line has been
only lightly used by new owner
Norfolk Southern (which inherited
the line from Conrail) and the
NYS&W. Starrucca is a majestic
landmark from the early days of
railroading. The fact that more than
150 years after its completion it is
still in service is a tribute to its designers and builders, and it is a
rare privilege to watch a train rum-
ble across the great bridge.

Above: In this glass-plate view from about 1910, an Erie camelback leads an eastbound Erie freight across Starrucca Viaduct. Compare this photo with the view made roughly 50 years later of a diesel powered Erie-Lackawanna freight.

Opposite page: On October 29, 1961, an eastbound Erie-Lackawanna freight climbing toward Gulf Summit crosses Starrucca. Leading the train is a former Erie Railroad Electro Motive Division F3A followed by an FTB and FTA.

Jim Shaughnessy

Tunkhannock Viaduct

An empty coal train run by Canadian Pacific's Delaware & Hudson and led by Norfolk Southern diesels rolls over the former Delaware, Lackawanna & Western Tunkhannock Viaduct at Nicholson, Pennsylvania. Modern railroading in the Northeastern United States reflects more than 40 years of mergers, consolidations, and line abandonment. While the DL&W connected Hoboken, New Jersey (across the Hudson from New York City) and Buffalo, New York, today this bridge on a portion of the old Lackawanna serves as north-south line on Canadian Pacific's route between Montreal, Albany, and Harrisburg.

Looming large above the village of Nicholson, Pennsylvania, is the colossal neo-Roman Tunkhannock Viaduct. This great bridge, named for the Tunkhannock Creek Valley it spans, was the largest reinforced-concrete bridge in the world when it was completed in 1915, and it remains the largest of its style. This gargantuan bridge seems out of proportion with its surroundings. It is nearly one-half mile long (2,375 feet) and rises 240 feet over the valley floor, towering over the houses and shops in the village. The scale of the bridge dwarfs that of the trains that cross it, and observers from ground level are often surprised when they see a "tiny" train inch across the bridge. Yet these "tiny" trains are often heavy freights, more than 15 feet tall and a mile long!

The Tunkhannock Viaduct is one of the few remnants of the once great Delaware, Lackawanna & Western Railroad—a company that built its fortunes on the anthracite coal trade in eastern Pennsylvania and eventually expanded its reach from the New York metropolitan area to Buffalo, New York. The Lackawanna, as the line is known, was cobbled together from a host of short railroads, some of which were laid out using primitive engineering from the earliest days of American railroading. As a result, the railroad didn't follow the best possible path. This changed when William H. Truesdale became president of the railroad in 1899, and set out to vastly improve the property. Truesdale was an experienced railroad man who had learned his trade from the ground up. He had been employed in a variety of capacities by several different lines, and was well versed in the trade. He knew how to make the railroad better and wasted no time in implementing the latest technology on the Lackawanna.

Although the Delaware, Lackawanna & Western merged with the Erie in 1960, and since that time its main line has been largely fragmented, downgraded and abandoned, the sun has not set on the mighty Tunkhannock Viaduct. This bridge still hosts four to eight freights daily.

Among his crusades were the construction of new lines and modern facilities, such as a new Hoboken Terminal.

In 1908, Truesdale began construction of a significantly shorter route across western New Jersey. This was built to the most modern standards and featured a comparatively straight and level profile, using deep cuts, high fills, and two large reinforced concrete bridges. Upon its completion in 1911, Truesdale went ahead with a second major line relocation, the Nicholson or Clarks Summit-Hallstead Cutoff, which effectively rebuilt much of the DL&W's line over Clarks Summit railroad west (geographically north) of Scranton. This line change nipped just 3.6 miles off the older route, but more to the point, the Nicholson Cutoff significantly reduced the gradient and the curvature on this tough mountain crossing. This was required in order to speed up operations and dramatically increase capacity. The new line had a maximum ruling grade of just 0.6 percent (uncompensated for curvature), compared with 1.23 percent on the older alignment. The new line eliminated 60 percent of the curvature on the route. This low profile simplified the movement of freight trains, allowing for much less complex helper operations, and permitted the through assignment of freight locomotives from Scranton to terminal points beyond Binghamton. This was an especially important change, because it allowed for much more efficient equipment utilization. The Cutoff trimmed freight runs over Clark Summit by an hour or more, and passenger schedules were trimmed by 20 minutes.

Tunkhannock Viaduct was designed by DL&W's bridge engineer Abraham Burton Cohen, and had always been the most visible and most impressive aspect of the Nicholson Cutoff. The railroad was quick to boast about the bridge's superlative attributes, and it was often featured in company literature including public passenger schedules and brochures. The bridge is made of 10 vast arched spans, each 180 feet across. Enormous piers, one of which is set as far as 92 feet below ground in order to reach solid bedrock, support each arch. Some 167,000 cubic yards of concrete, and an estimated 1,140 tons of steel were used in the viaduct.

The Lackawanna was a busy and profitable railway through the first decades of the 20th century, but its fortunes waned as the anthracite business declined. Although the line was successfully adapted as a bridge line connecting New York, Buffalo, and the Great Lakes, it faced stiff competition from several other parallel carriers, including the New York Central, Lehigh Valley and Erie Railroad. By the mid 1950s, the line was in deep trouble and began consolidating its assets with its longtime rival, the Erie. The two lines served many of the same markets and had largely duplicative facilities in the New York Terminal area and west of Binghamton, New York. In 1960, the two companies merged, forming the Erie-Lackawanna. In 1976, this was one of several bankrupt carriers absorbed by the federally created Conrail system. The old Lackawanna route did not fare well during these consolidations and precious little of the railroad remains as mainline today (much of it west of Binghamton has been abandoned). The Nicholson Cut-off line between Scranton and Binghamton is one of the few segments of the old DL&W that still serves as a through freight corridor. It is now operated by the Canadian Pacific via its Delaware & Hudson subsidiary, and sees four to eight heavy freight trains daily.

Lackawanna's massive Tunkhannock Viaduct is comprised of 10 reinforced concrete arches that together span roughly one half mile across the valley of Tunkhannock Creek.

Rockville Bridge

On a hazy summer evening in July 1989, a pair of Conrail SD40-2s roll across the Rockville Bridge. When the bridge opened in 1902, the 4-4-0 American type was still common, and most freight trains were hauled by 2-8-0 Consolidations. Even the largest locomotives of the period seem like featherweights compared to an Electro-Motive SD40-2, yet the bridge can easily accommodate large modern diesels.

Building westward across its namesake state in the late 1840s, the Pennsylvania Railroad selected a broad, yet shallow crossing of the mighty Susquehanna River at Rockville, about five miles north of the state capital. Its first bridge here was a wooden, single-track structure that was nearly three-quarters of a mile long. This bridge served adequately until it was replaced by a more modern, double track iron structure in 1877. Despite the greater capacity of the new bridge, by 1900 the Pennsylvania Railroad had become one of the busiest transportation arteries in the United States, and was building a four-track main line between New York, Philadelphia, and Pittsburgh to accommodate the tremendous flow of freight and passenger traffic. At this time, it replaced numerous older bridges made of wood, iron, or steel with more traditional stone-arch structures to ensure greater durability.

The third bridge at Rockville was started in 1900, and opened to traffic in 1902. It is listed in the *Guinness Book of Rail Facts and Figures*, as "the world's largest stone arch railway bridge over a river." It consists of 48 stone arch spans. William D. Middleton notes in *Landmarks of the Iron Road* that the bridge is 3,820 feet long, and 52 feet wide. William S. Young explains that Rockville Bridge is faced with stone masonry, but the greater part of the bridge is made of concrete and rubble. Under the direction of William H. Brown, this form of construction was used by the PRR for a number of other bridges.

The Rockville Bridge originally carried four mainline tracks, but today the bridge has just three tracks as a result of infrastructure trimming in the Conrail period. There are junctions at both ends of the bridge, allowing it to serve several lines, and permitting freight trains to reach yards on both banks of the Susquehanna. Pennsylvania Railroad's gigantic Enola Yards, located a few miles south of the bridge on the west bank of the river was one of the largest railroad yards in the world in its heyday.

Today the 100-year-old bridge is owned by Norfolk Southern, the company that operates the former Pennsylvania main line across Pennsylvania, as well as PRR's Harrisburg to Buffalo route on the east bank of the Susquehanna. The Rockville Bridge is still a primary traffic corridor and numerous freight trains cross it every day, along with Amtrak's *Three Rivers*, and *Pennsylvanian*.

In July 1989, a Conrail SD40-2 leads an eastbound freight across the Rockville Bridge.

In October 2001, a Norfolk Southern auto-rack train crosses the Rockville Bridge, which spans the Susquehanna River a few miles north of Harrisburg, Pennsylvania.

Hoosac Tunnel

Jim Shaughnessy collection

Hoosac Tunnel operations were electrified from 1911 until 1946, making it one of the shortest-lived mainline electrifications in the United States. Electrics would haul steam powered trains—locomotive and all—through the tunnel in order to avoid the severe smoke problems that occurred when steam locomotives worked up grade through the bore. This view of a westbound train with an electric leading a Boston & Maine 2-6-0 Mogul dates from about 1920.

One of the great engineering works of the 19th century is the Hoosac Tunnel. Noteworthy for its early start, prolonged construction, and historical mystique, the Hoosac Tunnel was hailed as one of the wonders of its time. It seems ancient today, but the tunnel was the embodiment of technology, transportation, and progress when it was new. Its construction lasted for more than a generation, and for more than 40 years it was the longest tunnel in North America. It is 4.75 miles long (25,081 feet) and lies 1,718 feet below the western summit of Hoosac Mountain in the northwest corner of Massachusetts.

Follow the tracks westward along the Deerfield River through the rural towns of Shelburne Falls, Charlemont, and Zoar, and you will find yourself winding through a deep and narrowing valley that is ultimately boxed in by the towering mass of Hoosac Mountain. The east portal of the tunnel is located in the town of Florida, near a highway grade crossing. These days, passage of trains through the tunnel is infrequent, but if you have the luck, or the patience, you will be rewarded with one of most fascinating railway experiences New England can offer.

The stone-faced portal bears the date 1877, but the tunnel is even older than that. Beyond the portal is opaque blackness ... silent, foreboding, yet compelling. The tunnel comes alive when its blackness is pierced. The wall of darkness is struck ever so faintly by a distant glimmer. The uninitiated might assume that this light is the headlight of the approaching train, but it isn't. The tunnel is at the summit of the railroad, and the glimmer you see is the reflection of a locomotive's headlight on the roof of the tunnel. When a train passes the summit of the tunnel, located at roughly at the tunnel's midpoint, the

faint glimmer suddenly becomes a brightening twinkle. Soon the rush of musty, cool, damp air pushed forward by the mass of the freight rushes past you. Yet, for the moment, the tunnel remains silent, save for the unceasing dripping of water. Then, slowly ... the tunnel begins to utter a distant groaning that grows louder as the train approaches the portal. Now—stand clear! The train rushes forth, bursting from the oppressive bounds of the mountain to pursue its eastward journey down the valley of the Deerfield River. The machine roars onward, heading toward the East Deerfield Yards on the banks of the Connecticut River.

A tunnel below Hoosac Mountain was conceived in the 1820s as the path for a canal—then the transport mode of choice—but the idea lay dormant for a generation. The canal tunnel did not advance, and the completion of the Western Railroad of Massachusetts in 1841 spurred further interest in another railroad across the Berkshires, resulting in renewed interest in a long tunnel below the mountains. In 1848, the Troy and Greenfield Railroad was charted to connect Troy, New York (on the east bank of the Hudson River), with Greenfield, Massachusetts (in the Connecticut River Valley). One optimistic tunnel proponent suggested a tunnel could be bored under the mountain in less than five years. Optimism exceeded ability; more than two-and-a-half decades would pass before a tunnel was opened. At times it seemed an unending task; the prospects of the tunnel's completion appeared remote and costly. Over the years, tunnel construction was led by a variety of chief engineers who had to overcome serious geological, financial, and political hurdles before the first trains could roll below the mountains. The Hoosac Tunnel was one of the most discussed and controversial topics of the day.

The tunnel runs between Florida, Massachusetts, and the town of North Adams. Initial boring began in 1851 at the east portal. In 1852, one of the world's first tunnel-boring machines was put to work. The concept of a tunnel-boring machine was valid, and many of them have been used around the world, but this early effort failed about a dozen feet into the mountain. This initial attempt proved to be a false start. When boring finally resumed, a new east portal was started just a few hundred feet from the first.

In 1856, Hermann Haupt took over the Hoosac Tunnel project. He was a former chief engineer of the Pennsylvania Railroad, and had worked with J. Edgar Thomson on that line's Allegheny crossing (see pages 106 to 109). Haupt made some progress with the Troy & Greenfield line itself, but despite his earlier engineering accomplishments, the tunnel got the best of him. He failed to secure sufficient financial backing,

When Boston & Maine dieselized its Fitchburg main line, electric operations through the Hoosac Tunnel were discontinued. A pair of Electro-Motive Division FTs and an F2A led a westbound freight at the west portal of the Hoosac Tunnel on September 10, 1955. At that time, the line through the tunnel was still double-tracked.

Jim Shaughnessy

and suffered from serious political opposition, but his primary difficulty was the lack of proper tools. The traditional tunneling methods of hand drills and black powder were not enough to conquer Hoosac Mountain. So after five frustrating years he gave up, having bored less than a mile of tunnel.

Following Haupt's departure and financial failure of the Troy & Greenfield Railroad, the Commonwealth of Massachusetts assumed control of the construction of the Hoosac Tunnel. Under state supervision, specialists traveled to Europe to study the construction of the Mt. Cenis Tunnel, a 7.6-mile transAlpine bore being built between France and Italy, which, when completed in

1871, became the longest tunnel in the world. Based on the Mt. Cenis work, pneumatic drills were developed for use on the Hoosac Tunnel. Drills were made locally in Greenfield, and ultimately proved more effective than the earlier drills. An equally important innovation occurred in 1867, when the tunnel builders employed a newly developed explosive called nitroglycerin in place of black powder. The combination of these new technologies greatly speeded tunneling. By the mid 1860s, it was felt a larger bore was needed in order to provide space for a double track line and larger railway cars. As a result, much of Haupt's work (which had only provided for just a single track) was re-bored. Tunneling progressed from both the east and west portals as well as from interior faces reached by deep shafts dug from the surface. After the completion of the tunnel, these shafts were used for ventilation.

Finally, according to Carl R. Byron's *A Pinprick of Light*, on November 27, 1873, the mountain was bored through. More than a year passed, however, before the tracks were laid through the tunnel. The first train rolled through it to North Adams on February 9, 1875, while the first official passenger train passed through on October 13, 1875, and regular service commenced in the following months. To put it in a chronological perspective, the Hoosac Tunnel took longer to build than the entire survey and construction of the nation's first transcontinental railroad, which had spanned half a continent by May 1869.

The Hoosac Tunnel route quickly developed as a primary transportation artery. The Commonwealth of Massachusetts operated the tunnel initially, and charged a toll for trains passing through it. Several different railroads built lines in the direction of the Hoosac in anticipation of access. However, most of these schemes stopped far short of the tunnel. On the west side of the tunnel, two lines were built: One to Troy, New York, and the other to Rotterdam Junction by way of Mechanicville, New York. Although parallel east of Johnsonville, New York, these lines were not on adjacent alignments, and in places were separated by a mile or more. In the 1880s, the Fitchburg Railroad bought the tunnel from Massachusetts as part of a consolidation of the east-west Hoosac Tunnel route. It combined the two parallel western lines and operated them as a double track route. (This unusual paired track arrangement survived until the 1970s, when one route was abandoned.) By the 1880s, growing traffic required a second track through the tunnel, finally making use of the extra space provided.

The Fitchburg Railroad was absorbed by the Boston & Maine Railroad in 1900. The Boston & Maine gradually pieced together a regional railway network that ultimately blanketed much of northern New England. The Hoosac Tunnel suffered from capacity constraints as a result of residual locomotive smoke inside the bore. Since the tunnel is the railroad's mountain summit, trains in both directions have to work upgrade. In steam days, this resulted in terrible smoke problems as locomotives worked hard in the confined space of the tunnel, completely filling it with suffocating smoke.

A number of different ideas were tried to minimize the smoke in the tunnel. The most effective occurred in 1910 when the Boston & Maine came under common management with the New Haven Railroad. The New Haven had pioneered America's first large scale mainline electrification scheme for its New York area suburban services. One advantage of electrification was the

Although the Hoosac Tunnel is still used as a main line, it is not the busy place it had been in its glory years. At one time, there was as many as 100 movements a day through the tunnel; today just four to eight trains pass through it. The amount of support infrastructure around the tunnel is greatly diminished and, since the end of the electric era, trees have closed in around the tunnel portals. Compare this October 2000 photo of a westbound Guilford freight with the Jim Shaughnessy view made 45 years earlier.

elimination of steam locomotives and their consequent smoke problem. Using the high-voltage overhead technology developed by the New Haven, B&M electrified its tunnel operation by May 1911.

But the advent of practical commercial diesel-electric motive power resulted in the discontinuance of many American mainline line electrification schemes. So, while the Hoosac was one of the first mainline tunnel electrification schemes implemented, it was also among the first to be discontinued. The Boston & Maine took advantage of Electro-Motive's pioneering FT freight locomotive, receiving its first units in 1943. With the arrival of passenger diesels in 1946, B&M no longer had a practical need for maintaining complex electric operations through the Hoosac Tunnel as the diesel electrics did the job adequately.

The postwar years saw the rapid decline of the Hoosac Tunnel route. Freight and passenger traffic dropped off sharply after the war. In 1957, the B&M single-tracked the line through the tunnel in order to improve clearances for trailers on flatcar "piggy back" intermodal services. A year later, regular passenger services were discontinued. Railroads in the eastern United States were in serious financial trouble by the late 1960s, and in the 1970s, the B&M was one of several bankrupt lines—although it managed to stay out of the Conrail consolidation that absorbed several large eastern carriers. B&M emerged from bankruptcy in 1983 and was melded with the Maine Central under Guilford Transportation.

At first, the Hoosac Tunnel route prospered under Guilford, but in 1990 the majority of the east-west traffic that passed through the Hoosac was shifted to Conrail's route over the Boston & Albany via Worcester. For nearly a decade after that, only a trickle of traffic passed through the tunnel, consisting mostly of coal trains, and a bit of interchange traffic from the Delaware & Hudson. In 1998, Guilford arranged for the enlargement of the Hoosac Tunnel to accommodate both double stacks and tri-level covered auto carriers. With the break up of Conrail in 1999, traffic through the Hoosac Tunnel has nearly returned to pre-1990 levels; as of this writing in 2002, three to four trains traverse the line daily in each direction.

Boston & Maine's Hoosac Tunnel electrification was based on the New Haven's, and energized at 11,000 volts alternating current. B&M box cab electrics were built by Baldwin-Westinghouse, patterned after a New Haven design. This pair is seen framed by the east portal of the tunnel in December 1912.

Tehachapi

Santa Fe's 991 train is just a thin streak of red and silver against the pastoral spring setting of the Tehachapis. This train, led by no less than eight locomotives dressed in Santa Fe's attractive "Warbonnet" livery, approaches Bealville, California, on its tough climb from Caliente to Tehachapi Summit. Santa Fe had trackage rights over Southern Pacific through the Tehachapi Mountains.

California's Tehachapi Mountains straddle the Sierra Nevada and Coast Ranges, creating a barrier between the Central Valley and the Mojave Desert. The Tehachapis appear deceivingly benign to the untrained eye. Unlike the rocky, snow covered peaks, and steep slopes of the Swiss Alps, the Colorado Rockies, or the nearby Sierra Nevada, the north slopes (or west slope on the railroad) of the Tehachapis are characterized by rolling, grassy hills, punctuated by neatly placed oaks. Yet there is always the foreboding backdrop of tougher, higher, rockier ground beyond. What eludes most photographs of the area, and defies adequate description, is the underlying verticality of the Tehachapis.

Beauty is the beast of these mountains. The exquisite scenery here has made for some of the most difficult railroading in the world. Every day, for the last one and a quarter centuries, the Tehachapi crossing has tried railroad managers. On most days, navigating the crossing is just a matter of moving a large number of long, heavy freights over one of the world's most difficult passes. But at other times, it has meant attempting to counter the most violent forces of nature; this is volatile terrain, and on several occasions terrible floods and earthquakes have destroyed the railroad. Despite its challenges, Tehachapi remains one of the busiest railroad passes in the western United States, and it is certainly one of the most interesting to observe in action. As a veteran railroader and railroad photographer once said, "Tehachapi is the greatest train watchin' place in the world."

Southern Pacific conquered Tehachapi in the 1870s as the railroad was building eastward from the Sacramento area toward New Orleans by way of Los Angeles. The Southern Pacific, as its name suggests, was chartered to serve as the southerly transcontinental railroad, just as the Central Pacific had taken a central route, and the Northern Pacific would take a northerly course. By the time the SP started to build its line, the company had come under the control of the "Big Four"—Leland Stanford, Collis P. Huntington, Charles Crocker, and Mark Hopkins—the principals behind the Central Pacific. The Central Pacific built their line over Donner Pass and across the Nevada desert to meet the Union Pacific at Promontory, thus forming the first transcontinental line. Under the Big

Four, Central Pacific and Southern Pacific became inextricably intertwined in a Byzantine complexity of corporate entanglements that were eventually known colloquially as just the SP.

A brilliant young engineer named William Hood laid out the line over the Tehachapis. A Civil War veteran and Dartmouth college graduate, Hood had made his way west to seek his fortune. While he surveyed most of the SP route between Lathrop, California, and San Antonio, Texas, it is the spectacular Tehachapi crossing that earned him the most praise. His line starts its ascent near Bakersfield, California, but the most serious climb begins at Caliente. From this point, Hood's alignment follows a steep, sinuous profile that winds through a succession of tight Horseshoe and reverse curves in its climb up the

These three views were all made from the same hilltop above Tunnel 2 on March 28, 1992 in the California Tehachapis. In the first photo, an eastbound Santa Fe freight is seen climbing near Tunnel 1, railroad direction east of Caliente. In the second two photos, another eastbound freight climbs through old Allard on its way toward Bealville. The train is visible on two levels of track in the second photo in this sequence, illustrating how the railroad winds its way up through the mountains. The idyllic California scenery, sinuous track arrangement, and constant parade of long freight trains makes Tehachapi one of the greatest places to watch and photograph trains in the world.

mountain. By following the contours of the land, and using short tunnels, cuts, and fills where necessary, Hood was able to keep the gradient to a maximum of 2.2 percent (a 2.2 foot climb for every hundred feet traveled). The seven miles of track between Caliente and the siding at Cliff gain the railroad a little more than one mile distance as the crow flies, but lifts the line more than 700 feet. Further up the line at Walong, Wood laid out his best-known section of track, the world's first complete railroad spiral which is used to gain 77 feet elevation, while keeping to the 2.2 gradient. At the center of this spiral—universally known as the Tehachapi Loop—is the ninth of 17 tunnels built between Bakersfield and Tehachapi Summit. The famous loop is near the town of Keene, ten miles from Tehachapi summit.

Tehachapi station sits at an elevation of 3,967 feet above sea level, while the railroad crests the grade at 4,028 feet, having climbed 2,737 feet from Caliente. From the summit, the line drops down a steep, but less tortuous, line to the town of Mojave. SP reached Tehachapi Summit in July 1876, and the line was completed through to Los Angeles by September. Southern Pacific's Sunset Route to New Orleans finally opened in January 1883.

William Hood enjoyed a long and productive career with the Southern Pacific, eventually becoming the line's Chief Engineer. He is credited for engineering many of the SP's most difficult grades, including its especially steep and twisting Siskiyou Crossing on the California-Oregon border, and the Coast Line route over Cuesta near San Luis Obispo. Although Hood was the first to design and build a circular loop, he was not the last. This device has only been used a few times in the United States, yet it has found numerous applications on mountain lines around the world—the more prominent examples being Canadian Pacific's Spiral Tunnels on Kicking Horse Pass, and on several Swiss Alpine crossings.

The term "loop" can prove misleading in a railroad context, as many so-called loops do not actually form a complete circle. For example, the Arnold Loop at Silver Zone Pass on the old Western Pacific route near the Nevada-Utah state line only curves around about three-quarters of circle, making a tight horseshoe, or hairpin turn, rather than a complete circle. (Yet the William's Loop farther west does make a complete spiral like the Tehachapi Loop.) Furthermore, in British railway terminology, a "loop" is what Americans would call a "passing siding," in other words, a short section of track with connections to the main line at both ends to allow trains to meet or overtake one another.

Until 1899, Southern Pacific had the Tehachapis to itself, but this exclusivity ended when the Santa Fe desired a through-line to the Bay Area. By this time Santa Fe had already completed a line from the east, and had acquired a route through the Central Valley. Although anxious to keep out competition, SP negotiated with Santa Fe and agreed to provide the company trackage rights over its Tehachapi crossing. Southern Pacific granted Santa Fe joint access to its Tehachapi crossing between Mojave and Bakersfield. While Santa Fe split maintenance costs with SP and had equal running rights over the line, ownership and operations remained an SP domain. Had Santa Fe been denied access to SP's mountain crossing, John Signor, in his book, *Tehachapi*, explains, that it had plans to construct its own equally sinuous mountain line by way of Tejon Creek. In 1995, Santa Fe merged with Burlington Northern to form Burlington Northern Santa Fe, while in 1997, SP was absorbed into the Union Pacific system. Today Union Pacific operates the Tehachapi crossing, and BNSF utilizes the rights it inherited from Santa Fe.

Despite very heavy traffic, the Tehachapis' rugged topography has precluded complete double tracking of the line, and significant portions of the west slope remain a single track operation with intermittent passing sidings. Since two heavily traveled railroads come together for an especially difficult mountain crossing, the Tehachapis is a traffic choke point. The steep grades, and sharp

curves pose severe speed restrictions, which greatly limit capacity. Furthermore, since many trains require helpers to make it over the mountain (helpers are extra locomotives used in graded territory), operations are slowed as helpers are added and removed from trains, while capacity is further restrained because once a helper set has brought a train over the mountain, it needs to return "light engine" (without a train). Over the years, helper operations have offered a fascinating display of motive power. The extreme curvature precluded the use of excessive amounts of power at either the front or the back of the train. In steam days, it was common to find four or five locomotives, each with its own crew, spaced throughout a heavy freight train. Although diesel operations simplified helper operations, the Tehachapis have remained one of the few places where mid-train helpers are still a common occurrence. Southern Pacific routinely assigned two sets of helpers to its especially heavy coal trains crossing Tehachapi from mines in Utah, destined for a power plant in Trona, California.

The Tehachapi crossing has long been a preferred route for freight, although passenger trains also used the route until the advent of Amtrak in 1971. Now the line is devoid of passenger service despite its exceptional scenery and strategic location; Amtrak operates trains on a former Santa Fe routing from the Bay Area to Bakersfield, and provides through services to Los Angeles via the old SP Coast Line.

Southern Pacific's SNTA-C, a unit coal train that operated from the Skyline Mine in Utah to Trona, California, crosses over itself at Walong. This heavy train required three sets of locomotives; the lead locomotives are on top, the mid-train helpers are out of sight, and the rear-end helpers are about to enter Tunnel 9 at the center of the Tehachapi Loop.

Brian Jennison made this classic view of the Tehachapi loop on February 1, 1976. A clean Santa Fe SD40-2 leads a westbound train at Walong. The spiral arrangement of the loop enabled photographers to capture both the head-end and rear-end of a train in the same photo.

The Tehachapis are now the domain of Union Pacific, which acquired the Southern Pacific in 1996; BNSF also uses the line via trackage rights inherited from the Santa Fe. On November 30, 2001, an eastbound Union Pacific freight ascends the famous Tehachapi Loop at Walong, California.

Mike Gardner

Forth Bridge

The cantilever sections of the Firth of Forth Bridge are reached by long viaducts from each shore of the estuary. This photo was made from South Queensferry, which can be easily reached from Edinburgh by train or bus.

To have stood on the southern banks of that great Scottish estuary, the Firth of Forth, and imagined a bridge across it required enormous vision. To have drafted a plan for such a bridge took courage and wisdom. And to actually execute such a vision required great skill, labor—and lots of money. The first vision of a bridge over the Firth of Forth dates to the romantic Regency Era: in 1818, James Anderson of Edinburgh proposed such a crossing. A more serious proposal was suggested by Sir Thomas Bouch in 1872. Although his project was approved, delays in the construction dragged out for seven years. In the meantime, Bouch designed and built a two-mile long bridge across the Firth of Tay—another great sea inlet of the east side of Scotland. However, when Bouch's Tay Bridge was destroyed by a fierce storm in 1879, taking with it a loaded train of 78 passengers—all of whom perished—his pending Firth Bridge proposal was discredited and abandoned.

Yet the need for a bridge across the Firth of Forth outweighed fears of another bridge disaster and more proposals were developed. The best proposal was put forth by Sir John Fowler and Sir Benjamin Baker, who presented a plan for a magnificent cantilever bridge to span the tidal water of the Firth of Forth. Baker was a proponent of the cantilever, an ancient bridge design that had come into fashion again with the recent construction of a bridge over the River Main in Germany. Fowler and Baker overcame great difficulties in designing a bridge to span the Firth of Forth. In addition to the distance across the estuary, the bridge needed to accommodate the passage of sea-going sailing ships, which meant at least 150 foot clearance from the bottom of the bridge to the top of the water during the highest tides. A more serious concern,

Like the iron skeleton of a giant dinosaur, the Firth of Forth Bridge spans its namesake tidal estuary. The bridge is used by trains operating from Edinburgh to the north of Scotland.

especially in light of the Tay Bridge disaster, was the effect of wind on the Forth Bridge. This area is notorious for its fierce weather and is sometimes set upon by very powerful winds. Baker initiated a series of wind measurements and experiments near the site of the bridge to assist in its design.

The cantilever plan was drafted in 1881 and was approved by Parliament in 1882. Work on the bridge began in 1883 and progressed for more than six years. More than 5,000 men were employed in construction, and at times as many as 4,000 were working on it simultaneously. Three gigantic cantilever towers were constructed; each is named for the area where it was built. The southern most tower is Queensferry, for the town on the southern shore of the Forth; the central tower and the largest of the three, is Inchgarvie, after the island that it rests on; the northern tower is called Fife, after the county on the northern bank of the Forth. Each tower has four piers, each of which was sunk using a pneumatic caisson. (A pneumatic caisson permits men to work under higher than normal air pressure, and requires an air lock to allow the workers in and out of the site safely.) Some piers reach down as far as 90 feet below water. Each pier supports a massive steel tube, 12 feet in diameter, that rises 324 feet into the air. The tubes are arranged in a roughly pyramidal structure 120 feet apart at the base, and 33 feet apart at the top of the tower. Viewing the cantilever portion in profile reveals its symmetrical construction. Between the towers are two suspended sections, each measuring 350 feet long. Each of the outside towers connects with an approach viaduct on one end, while supporting half of a suspended section on the other. The Inchgarvie middle tower, which is slightly longer than the outside towers, supports suspended sections on both ends. An intricate maze of steel lattice is built around the basic cantilever structure to strengthen it and provide the needed support the engineers believed was required to withstand very high winds. A viaduct crosses within this steel maze to support the double track railway line. The cantilever section of the bridge is 5,350 feet long, and the entire bridge, including approach viaducts, is 8,296 feet long (1.5 miles), making it by far the largest bridge of its generation.

The Forth Bridge was formally completed on March 4, 1890, when the Prince of Wales, later to become King Edward VII, ceremonially drove the last rivet. The amount of material involved in the bridge is astounding, and a listing gives one a sense of its immensity: More than 60,400 tons (2,000 lbs. per U.S. ton) of steel was used, including more than 6.5 million rivets (some reports indicate as many as 8 million rivets). Since there are slightly more than 5 million people in Scotland, it is safe to say there are more rivets in the Firth of Forth Bridge than there are residents in Scotland!

Modern engineers believe that Baker and Fowler over-designed the bridge; it is much stronger than it needs to be to withstand even the most severe winds and weather. No doubt the Forth Bridge's engineers felt it safer to err on the side of caution and build a far stronger bridge than need be, than risk another disaster along the lines of the Tay Bridge. Its great strength permitted trains to cross it at speeds of up to 40 mph, an unusual characteristic for such a large bridge; many such bridges of the period would have been saddled with severe speed restrictions needed to keep locomotives from pounding the structure to pieces.

Despite its immensity, this massive steel bridge suffers from corrosion. Salty sea breezes perpetually assault the bridge and unless maintenance forces are vigilant, its structural integrity would quickly be undermined by rust and decay. The bridge has 135 acres of steel surface that requires more than 60 U.S. tons of paint to cover it, and painting the bridge is a never-ending task. As the story goes, a small army of full-time painters is employed year round, as it takes approximately three years to completely cover the bridge. It is said that as soon as the painters reach one end of the bridge, it is time to begin again at the other end.

Today the Firth of Forth Bridge still carries freight and passenger trains rolling to the north of Scotland from Edinburgh. For more than 110 years this magnificent structure has loomed high over the waters for which it is known. It is one of the most impressive, and certainly one of the most famous railway bridges ever built.

A ScotRail passenger train rolls across the Firth of Forth Bridge at South Queensferry, Scotland.

Swiss Alpine Engineering

The *Bernina Express* ascends the Albula Gorge on the Rhätische Bahn near Bergün, Switzerland. A few minutes before this photo was made, the train traversed the tracks seen to the right of the locomotive. The twisting, sinuous nature of this mountain railway results in trains zigzagging their way up the mountain.

Switzerland has the greatest concentration of intense mountain railways in the world. Here railway engineers used every engineering tool available in the construction of tracks through the exceptionally difficult Alpine terrain. Rugged mountain peaks, deep gorges, and glaciers are the rule, and level, tangent running is infrequent and hard to come by. These Alpine railways reach places that conventional railway engineering might have deemed impractical, if not impossible, using conventional steel wheel technology. Skillful engineers laid out cleverly planned alignments that incorporated loops, spirals, tall viaducts and bridges, and long curving tunnels. In addition to designing some of the steepest adhesion railways in the world, in places where strict adhesion is not practical, rack railways are employed to lift trains up precipitously steep gradients.

Spectacular Narrow Gauge Network

The most interesting Alpine railways are part of the spectacular narrow gauge network in Southeastern Switzerland. This is a system of routes operated by three different railway companies that straddle the Alpine headwaters of three principal European rivers: the Rhein (Rhine), Rhône, and Danube. Despite a non-conforming gauge, difficult terrain, high altitudes and, at times, very deep snow, these railways are heavily traveled.

Narrow gauge lines have lower construction cost and permit railway construction in places where conventional standard gauge lines may prove prohibitively expensive. Mountain railways are often ideally suited to narrow gauge because it allows for smaller trains,

tighter curves, and steeper grades than standard gauge tracks. The requirement for smaller tunnels and cuts also produces cost savings.

The narrow gauge movement started in the 1870s and by the late 1880s, the narrow gauge fever had reached the mountainous region of southeastern Switzerland. Narrow gauge had been

used very effectively in the Rocky Mountains of Colorado and New Mexico. While the Rocky Mountain lines used three-foot gauge tracks, Swiss railways adopted meter gauge (three feet 3.4 inches) for their lines. Some of these narrow gauge lines are among the last major railway routes constructed in Switzerland.

Rhätische Bahn

The Rhätische Bahn (Rhaetian Railways) operates both the oldest and the newest portions of this narrow gauge network. It has several different routes, and is the longest of the three narrow gauge railways in the network. Rhätis-

One of the Rhätische Bahn's historic "Baby Crocodiles" (class Ge6/61) descends the Albula line near Bergün. These classic jack-shaft electrics were once standard motive power on this route.

che Bahn's mainline over the Albula Pass connecting Chur and St. Moritz is one of the most scenic railways in the world. One of its scenic highlights is the famous Landwasser Viaduct, a sharply curved stone arch bridge that crosses 230 feet above the Landwasser River on six semicircular spans. One of these six spans rests on the cliff side of a tremendous vertical precipice, while the railway tunnels into the cliff side after crossing the bridge. From an engineering perspective, probably the most fascinating portion of Rhätische Bahn is the circuitous stretch from Bergün to Preda in the Albula Gorge. Here the railway ascends 1,368 feet in just 3.75 air miles, requiring a steeply graded serpentine route 7.75 rail miles in length. It's a virtual spaghetti bowl of track that has thrilled tourists and railway enthusiasts since it opened to traffic in 1904. This short stretch of line climbs at 3.5 percent (a 3.5 feet ascent for every 100 feet traveled) through several spiral tunnels and over tall stone viaducts as it completes three complete loops on its way up the gorge. The track layout is sufficiently complex to disorient travelers as they wind their way up the mountain, and can even confuse a well-trained enthusiast on the ground carrying a detailed map of the line! At Preda, the railway plunges into the 3.75 mile long Albula Tunnel where the line crests at just under 6,000 feet above sea level.

The sinuosity of the Rhätische Bahn's Albula Pass crossing makes the SP's tortuous Tehachapi climb seem like a mere kink in the tracks. Originally this fantastic railway was operated with steam locomotives. Watching a narrow gauge steam locomotive battling the grades from Bergün to Preda must have been one of the greatest thrills for a locomotive enthusiast, but regular

steam power was short lived here. The advent of practical mainline electrification quickly put an end to regular steam operations. The Albula Pass crossing was electrified in 1919, and the Rhätische Bahn was entirely electrically operated by 1922. Today there is a constant parade of electrically powered trains on the line using a 11 kV 16.7 Hz transmission system. Both freight and passenger trains use this main line, and often the single-track mountain railway, at capacity. Yet despite heavy traffic, steep grades, and enormous snowfall, the line usually operates with characteristically tight Swiss punctuality. Swiss railways are as famous for their timekeeping as they are for the scenery they traverse.

Another especially spectacular portion of the Rhätische Bahn is its Bernina Line, (operated by a separate company known, until 1943, as the Bernina Railway), which connects the Swiss resort of St. Moritz with the Italian town of Tirano located on the Swiss-Italian frontier. This railway was built between 1908 and 1910 and was electrified from the time of construction. It crosses over its namesake pass, 7,400 feet high, and descends 6,000 feet through the Poschiavo Valley to reach Tirano, located 1,405 feet above sea level. This is among the most steeply graded adhesion railways in the world, with maximum gradients of 7.1 percent. By comparison, the world's first mountain railway, the Western Railroad of Massachusetts (now CSX's Boston Line) has a maximum grade of 1.67 percent, while the Central Pacific's pioneering Donner Pass crossing (now Union Pacific) has a maximum grade of 2.4 percent, and Rio Grande's narrow gauge Cumbres Pass crossing (now operated by the Cumbres & Toltec Scenic) features grades of four percent. At Tirano, passengers can con-

A Rhätische Bahn passenger train descends toward Bergün. Three levels of track can been seen in this image. In just a few minutes, the train will be on the tracks seen above the train, and then it will stop at Bergün station visible in the upper left.

tinue their journey on the Italian railways, giving the Swiss narrow gauge network the distinction of being the highest through railway in Europe.

The most recent portion of the Rhätische Bahn is its Vereina Line that opened on November 19, 1999. This line is located almost entirely in tunnels, including its namesake bore, 19.1 km long. This new route provides an Alpine link between Klosters (on Rhätische Bahn's route between Filisur and Lanquart) and Sagliains (on the line to Scuol). It was built in place of a new road over the mountains and like some other Alpine routes, handles car-ferry trains, allowing motorists a short cut through the mountains. Car ferries are especially valuable in the winter when many high mountain roads are closed because of deep snow.

The Rhätische Bahn near Bergün features a snaking, winding line that curves around many times on its seven-mile journey to Preda. Two levels of track can be seen here. Despite the tortuous nature of the railway and the single-track, narrow gauge operation, the Rhätische Bahn is a very heavily traveled line.

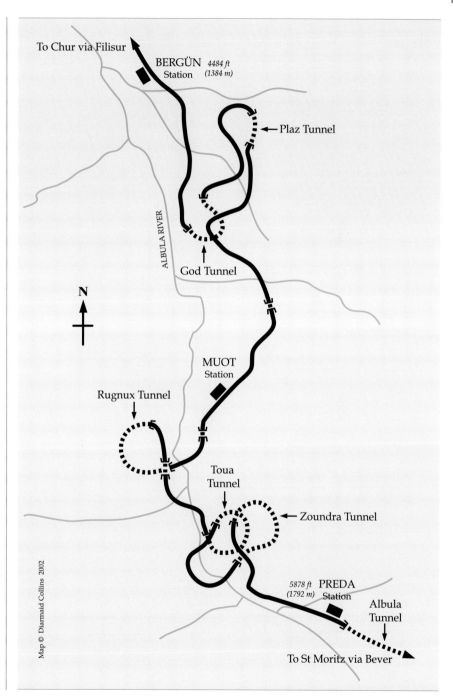

Route of the *Glacier Express*

One of the most scenic train rides in world is the highly acclaimed *Glacier Express*. Since 1930, it has operated from St. Moritz in the eastern part of Switzerland to Zermatt in the far western part of the country, over portions of all three of the Alpine narrow gauge railways. Westbound, the train crosses the Albula Pass, winds along the narrow gorge of the headwaters of the Rhine, and then up to Disentis. From there it uses the Furka-Oberalp Bahn to Brig. This steeply graded railway is named for the two high mountain passes that it crosses. The F-O route was one of the last through railways built in Switzerland. World War I delayed its construction and the line was not completed until 1926. Originally, the line was steam powered, but was electrified between 1940 and 1942. Unlike the Rhätische Bahn, the Furka-Oberalp Bahn does not rely on normal adhesion to get its trains over the mountains. With mainline grades as steep as 11 percent, the railway uses the Abt rack system, which is a centrally located, notched track that is engaged by a cog on the locomotive. The rack is only employed on the steepest track sections. Locomotives engage the rack at speed so the train does not need to stop climbing the mountain. The highest point on the Furka-Oberalp is Oberalp Pass, 6,667 feet (2033 meters) above sea level. Descending from Oberalp Pass, the line negotiates a sinuous sequence of horseshoe curves that zigzag down the mountain to Andermatt. Standing at the station in Andermatt, you can see a westbound train winding its way down what seems like an exceptional flight of stairs. Andermatt sits almost directly

An eastbound Furka-Oberalp Bahn train climbs to Feisch, located in a high Alpine valley. This line is so steeply graded that a conventional adhesion railway is impractical, so a central rack is engaged to lift trains up the toughest sections.

above the Swiss Federal Railways St. Gotthard Tunnel. A 2.5-mile (4 km) Furka Oberalp Bahn branch connects Andermatt with the village of Göschenen at the northern portal of the famous tunnel. This branch line descends on a phenomenally steep 17.9 percent grade through a series of snowsheds and tunnels that makes for one of the most fantastic short railway journeys in the world.

To the west of Andermatt, the Furka Oberalp Bahn main line climbs over Furka Pass. Until 1982, this line took a route that received such heavy snow, that it was routinely closed during the winter and certain key structures along the line, such as bridges, were removed to prevent damage from avalanches. Today the F-O traverses the 9.5 mile (15.4 km) long Furka-Basistunnel circumventing the most difficult portions

of the line. It is the second longest narrow gauge tunnel in the world following the Rhätische Bahn's Vereina Tunnel and, like that tunnel, the Furka-Basistunnel hosts a transalpine car ferry. Portions of the original Furka Pass line are now seasonally operated as a tourist railway. Brig is the western terminus of the Furka-Oberalp Bahn, and the junction with the BVZ Zermatt-Bahn, the narrow gauge line that hosts the *Glacier*

Express, and other services among its namesake towns of Brig, Visp, and Zermatt. Like the Furka Oberalp Bahn, this railway uses the Abt rack system on its steepest sections, as much as 12.5 percent gradients. Between Visp and Zermatt, the railway ascends 3,200 feet. Although Zermatt is the western end of the narrow gauge system, and the last stop for the *Glacier Express,* it is not necessarily the end of the railway journey. The Gornergrat Bahn starts at Zermatt and ascends to an elevation of 10,235 feet, using a rack-equipped line that climbs a 20 percent grade. This was one of the first railways in the world that was electrified using a three-phase alternating current system; however, the Gornergrat is more famous for its spectacular views of the Matterhorn than its unusual electrification.

The narrow gauge lines described here, while among the most spectacular, are just a few of the many wonderful Alpine railways operating in Switzerland. Many books have been written detailing the construction, operations, and scenic interludes of Swiss Railways.

The Rhätische Bahn ascends the Albula Gorge using a series of spiral tunnels to gain elevation. A train bound for St. Moritz crosses a viaduct that will take it across the gorge; below it is the south portal of the Toua Tunnel, which the train entered less than two minutes prior to its ascent to Preda.

Kate Shelley Bridge

Text by John Gruber

The Kate Shelley Bridge crosses the Des Moines River four miles west of Boone, Iowa. On a June 1996 evening, a long Union Pacific Powder River unit coal train rolls eastward across the bridge. The Chicago & North Western main line between Chicago and Council Bluffs has long served as a conduit for Union Pacific traffic from the West, and in 1995, North Western merged with Union Pacific.

The massive Kate Shelley Bridge over the Des Moines River on Union Pacific's busy east-west line is in an unlikely Midwestern location—west-central Iowa. When built, it was the world's longest and highest double track railroad bridge.

The Chicago & North Western opened the 2,685-foot viaduct to traffic on May 19, 1901, as a part of a project to improve and shorten its Chicago-to-Omaha main line. The railroad, which bragged about its "best of everything" passenger service, also engineered the biggest and best structures.

The bridge, four miles west of Boone, Iowa, is 185 feet high. Except for the river span of 300 feet, the structure consists of two bent, braced towers of 45 feet with intermediate spans of 75 feet carried by plate girders.

Construction started in the fall of 1899 on what was called the Boone-Ogden cut-off, an effort to shorten the main line and eliminate steep grades, which required extra engines for heavier trains. Instead of going down into the river valley, crossing on a low-level bridge, and climbing out of the valley, the railroad built the high bridge straight west from the Boone station. The new line was four miles shorter.

To begin, the C&NW built a temporary pile bridge to transport material from one side of the river to the other, as all material was unloaded on the east side of the river. The end abutments are stone masonry over concrete footings. The stone piers upon which the towers rest are built on rock, hardpan, or some other equally hard foundation. The river span, which is of the subdivided Pratt truss type, is supported on A-towers resting on caissons 10 feet in diameter filled with concrete, and sunk pneumatically to bedrock.

The statistics, reported in *Railway and Engineering Review*, are impressive: "In the superstructure there are 5,680 tons of metal, and in the foundations 400 tons more, making the total weight of metal in the entire structure 6,080 tons. The cost of the bridge proper was $625,000, and the total cost, including the approaches, was $1,250,000. The building of the approaches involved some heavy earthwork, there being two embankments about 85 feet high across ravines 400 feet long, requiring the moving of 223,000 cubic yards of material," the Chicago trade journal said.

The relocation routed the main tracks away from the village of Moingona, site of 15-year-old Kate Shelley's heroic trek on the stormy night of July 6, 1881, to find help for the crew of a wrecked freight train and warn passenger trains of the disaster. For many years, the story of her exploit was used in an Iowa school reader. She worked a term as a schoolteacher, but had to return home to care for her mother, brother, and sisters. Later, she accepted a long-standing offer from the C&NW, and from October 1903 until her death on January 21, 1912, she served as agent at Moingena. She attended the ceremonies opening the new structure and, after her passing, the C&NW named the bridge in her honor.

The night in 1881 was not the only occasion when a heavy storm hit the Boone area. Sixteen cars of a piggyback train were blown off the bridge on July 30, 1986, in a fierce rainstorm with high winds.

C&NW became a part of Union Pacific in 1995, and today, more than 100 years after its opening, the bridge is as busy as ever, carrying 65 to 80 trains a day—an enduring monument to C&NW engineering skill and a brave woman.

At dawn on June 9, 1996, the morning mists hang above the Des Moines River valley, as an eastbound Union Pacific freight rolls across the Kate Shelley High Bridge. Leading the train is a mix of locomotives painted for Chicago & North Western, Union Pacific, and Conrail.

Tulip Trestle

Text and photos by John Gruber

The former Illinois Central Tulip Trestle is located in Southwestern Indiana. This remarkable bridge hosts four to six trains daily. An Indiana Rail Road excursion crosses the bridge on September 30, 2000.

John Gruber

The Tulip Trestle in southwestern Indiana is in an unexpected, isolated location—an almost hidden valley in a state otherwise known for its vast expanses of flatland.

The 2,306-foot steel bridge, opened in 1906, takes its name from the nearby community of Tulip. Four to six trains daily cross the trestle used by the Indiana Rail Road, which took over operation from the Illinois Central in 1986. The freight line carries about eight million tons of coal annually, plus a wide variety of other traffic including household refrigerators, chemicals, petroleum productions, and building materials. An occasional passenger train also operates over the bridge.

The bridge is impressive. It is 161 feet above Richland Creek in Greene County. The approximate weight of the steel, furnished by the American Bridge Company, is 2,750 tons. The highest part of the structure is 112 feet from the base of rail to the top of the masonry. The bridge consists of two approach spans each 50 feet long, two approach spans each 60 feet long, 17 spans each 75 feet long, and 18 spans each 40 feet long. It is 19 track miles south of Bloomfield, 1-3/4 miles north of Tulip. Like other IC bridges, it was built for single track, "provision being made for double-tracking the bridge as soon as it becomes necessary," according to *Railway and Engineering Review*, Chicago. The bridge also is obscure, so obscure that it doesn't rate a mention in Richard J. Cook's *The Beauty of Railroad Bridges* (Golden West Books, 1987).

An IC subsidiary, the Indiana Southern, started to clear the land in the summer of 1905. Concrete pier and abut-

John Gruber

The Tulip Trestle carries the Indiana Rail Road 161 feet above Richland Creek.

ment work was completed on May 12, 1906. Construction started September 8, 1906, at the Bloomfield side and was completed November 22, 1906. The first train passed over the trestle on December 21, 1906.

Except for new rail and ties, little about the trestle has changed since its opening. Barrel stands constructed along the span to hold 55-gallon drums of water deteriorated, and have been removed. The water, to put out fires caused by steam locomotives, had not been needed since the IC dieselized the route in the early 1950s.

Like other railroad bridges, many local legends—some true, some obviously not true—surround the structure, according to the Bloomington *Sunday Herald-Times* in 1999: "There is, for example, the story of the construction worker who fell off the span but was saved by his new, rubber-soled boots when he hit the valley floor. Problem was, the guy kept bouncing up and down until his foreman had to shoot him to keep him from starving to death." The article was based on a fact-finding mission of Larry Shute, a fire chief, and *Herald-Times* environmental services manager.

Early in the 20th century, couples and families celebrated the Fourth of July by packing picnic baskets and going by cart, carriage, or automobile to the meadow below the trestle. Today, the land is farmed or overgrown with brush and wild grasses. Picnics, baseball games, and the other community activities ended a long time ago, but local people still drive along the winding country gravel road to admire the magnificent structure.

The Cascade Tunnels

Looking like a scene from Tolkien's *Lord of the Rings*, the abandoned concrete snowsheds of Great Northern's earlier Cascade crossing curve along the slopes of Cowboy Mountain. Tom Kline shot this vivid image on September 18, 1997.

Tom Kline

Under the direction of James J. Hill, John F. Stevens surveyed a northern transcontinental line from the Twin Cities of Minneapolis-St. Paul to Seattle in the 1880s and 1890s. This route was Hill's famed Great Northern, which was completed a generation after the first Transcontinental railroad to the Pacific. Unlike earlier transcontinental lines, Hill did not rely on massive public subsidy and land grants, and largely funded his efforts privately. Working his way west, John F. Stevens faced two challenging mountain ranges: The first was the Rockies, which he conquered relatively easily by way of Montana's Marias Pass (located near Glacier National Park); the second was the Washington Cascades, which proved far more difficult. Here, he located a narrow cleft in the mountains that would come to bear his name. From the outset, Stevens knew that a tunnel would be required for a properly graded line over the pass, but the construction of a long mountain tunnel would take longer to build than Hill had patience for—he wanted access to Pacific Northwest ports as quickly as possible. So to speed the Great Northern route to completion, Stevens forced a makeshift crossing over the pass that featured a ladder of switchbacks (a stub-end "V" arrangement of tracks used to gain elevation in a short distance, but which forces trains to back up, greatly slowing operations), and unacceptably steep four percent grades. By comparison, the rest of the line was built with a maximum gradient of just 2.2 percent, a standard climb in the western United States.

Complicating operations on the Stevens Pass crossing was extremely heavy snowfall, which often caused trains to bog down, and occasionally closed the line. Even when it wasn't snowing, a typical seven-car passenger

Above: The east portal of the original 2.5-mile Great Northern Cascade Tunnel. The white streaking is a result of lime leaching out of the century-old concrete.

Below: Great Northern's herald featured "Rocky" the mountain goat, symbolizing the wildlife that could be seen from the trains crossing Stevens Pass.

train weighing 500,000 lbs. would require not one, but three steam locomotives to scale the summit. Two would lead while one shoved on the rear. Travel across the line offered exceptional views, but was a slow, arduous journey. The steep climb and switchbacks created serious bottlenecks to operations; it was very expensive to operate and it would take hours for a train to negotiate the pass.

In 1900, the temporary line was closed in favor of a 2.6 mile-long summit tunnel that lowered the GN's Cascade Crossing by 677 feet, and shortened the distance over the pass by about nine miles. The new line was a vast improvement over the temporary crossing, but was still a bottleneck that was the bane of the operating department. The grade was kept to a 2.2 percent maximum and the switchbacks were eliminated, but the line navigated a looping, zigzag arrangement on the west slope using very tight horseshoe curves. The grade through the summit tunnel was limited to just 1.7 percent, yet operations through this long bore with steam locomotives was extremely difficult and dangerous. Locomotive engineers risked asphyxiation when working a heavy train up through the tunnel.

The line traversed some very dangerous terrain that passed directly through known avalanche runs. It was on this line that the famous Wellington Disaster occurred in 1910. Two passenger trains, which had been delayed by a Pacific storm, were making their way over Stevens Pass when they were swept into a ravine by a tremendous avalanche. More than a hundred people were killed, and it was one of the worst railway accidents in American history. Even when it wasn't snowing, moving trains over Stevens Pass was slow and difficult, and the climb to the summit tunnel greatly limited the capacity of the entire transcontinental route. In order to run heavier freight trains, the Great Northern was forced to innovate. It was one of the first lines in America to adopt the Mallet compound—massive, articulated locomotives using the double expansion principle for greater efficiency. Although first tried as helpers, GN soon assigned Mallet types to lead freights. It is believed that GN was the first American line to regularly use Mallets as lead locomotives. Using Mallets as leads proved more successful than double heading with 2-8-2 Mikados, but still didn't give GN the capacity it needed. In 1909, GN electrified its tunnel operations, using the then state-of-the-art three-phase alternating current system. The three-phase system offered great tractive effort, but involved an awkward transmission system that required two independent sets of wires. The electrification solved many of the problems associated with the summit tunnel, and effectively allowed Great Northern to triple its freight tonnage capacity over Stevens Pass, but electrification didn't help with the tremendous snowfall.

Finally, in 1925, the railroad decided to engineer a third line over Stevens Pass, and an elderly John F. Stevens directed the survey team to find the best possible crossing. A new tunnel, 7.8 miles long, was required, along with extensive line relocations to lower the crossing and avoid the most serious avalanche runs. The new summit tunnel was bored in record time, taking a little more than 37 months to complete. The tunnel was completed on December 28, 1928, and the new railroad officially opened on January 12, 1929. The second Cascade Tunnel is located between Berne and Scenic, Washington, and was the longest tunnel in North America on its completion. It is still the longest rail-

The abandoned remains of the east end concrete snowshed protecting the original Great Northern alignment at Tye, Washington, seen on September 18, 1997.

road tunnel in the United States, although the 9.1-mile tunnel built by Canadian Pacific on Rogers Pass, British Columbia in 1989 is now the longest railway tunnel on the continent.

In conjunction with the tunnel and line relocations, Great Northern decided to extend its electrification to cover the entire operating division from Wenatche to Skykomish, greatly simplifying operations. By this time, much progress had been made in the field of railroad elec-

trification, and GN's three-phase alternating current system was obsolete. GN re-electrified with a more modern, single-phase alternating current system. Like the Hoosac Tunnel electrification (see pages 120 to 124), GN's Cascade electrification was rendered unnecessary with the advent of dieselization. GN was slower to dieselize its tunnel operations than the Boston & Maine; the Cascade Tunnel retained its wires a decade longer than the Hoosac. Electric opera-

tions ended in 1956. The Great Northern route is now operated by Burlington Northern Santa Fe and is one of the busiest freight routes to the Pacific Northwest. Amtrak's daily *Empire Builder* also uses the line.

The second Cascade crossing, complete with tunnel and snowsheds, can still be traced by the more adventurous enthusiast. This line is on a substantially different alignment, running via Tye to the north of the 1929 tunnel.

Moffat Tunnel

Denver & Salt Lake No. 200, a 2-6-6-0 Mallet compound, exits the west portal of Moffat Tunnel shortly after the 6.1-mile bore was completed. Judging by the crowds, this may have been one of the first public trains to use the tunnel, which opened to traffic on February 26, 1928.

Denver Public Library Western History Department

Although known as the "Mile High City," Denver is not actually in the mountains. In reality, it sits on the edge of the Great Plains at the foot of the Rockies. Yet the mountains are not far away and the Front Range of the Rockies looms as an ominous barrier beyond the city to the west. These mountains foiled Denver's chances of being situated on a main transcontinental route for decades. The Union Pacific, when building the first transcontinental route, bypassed Denver to the north through Wyoming, while the Santa Fe followed a route to the south by way of New Mexico; even William Jackson Palmer's Rio Grande, although it started in Denver, ran well to the south before crossing the Rockies. Several railways started in Denver with grand ambitions of reaching to the west, but in the end, never made it any further than Colorado's lucrative mining districts. The last of these lines to be built was David H. Moffat's Denver, Northwestern & Pacific Railway.

Moffat was a Denver-based railway promoter whose life ambition seems to have been to put Denver on the main line of American commerce. Earlier railways had failed to achieve this goal, so in 1902, Moffat decided to build his line due west from Denver directly over the Front Range. In the short term, he planned to tap the Yampa Valley coal fields, but had his sights on connecting Denver and the Salt Lake via a direct line, and also as part of a much grander transcontinental scheme. Moffat funded much of the construction of the railway with his personal fortune.

Climbing through the Front Range, the line took a spectacular path over the top of Rollins Pass, reaching the lofty elevation of 11,660 feet, which made Moffat's railroad the highest mainline in North America. The highest portion of

The east portal of the Moffat Tunnel on July 23, 1995.

this route was viewed as a temporary line, and from the beginning, Moffat had intentions of building a tunnel through the Front Range. As a result, this section featured a grueling, tortuous profile with extremely sharp curves (as tight as 16 degrees) and long sections of four percent gradient—twice as steep as the rest of the line. The Rollins Pass crossing, known popularly as "The Giant's Ladder," was arguably the most scenic

line in America, and it was certainly the most difficult to operate. Snow fell at the highest elevations nine months of the year, and the winter conditions were especially severe. At times the line would be closed for days and even weeks because of heavy snow.

Moffat ran out of money in 1911 and died a short while later, leaving his dream unfulfilled. In 1913 the railroad was renamed the Denver & Salt Lake.

While Moffat's line reached the coal fields, it never progressed much further. The staggering cost of operating the Rollins Pass crossing absorbed most of the line's resources and the management of the railroad desperately sought relief through the construction of the tunnel through the Front Range.

In 1922, public funds were made available for the tunnel's construction and work began in 1923. The tunnel, named in Moffat's honor, was conceived of as both a railroad tunnel and a public aqueduct to channel water from the west side of the Front Range to Denver. In actuality, the Moffat is *two* tunnels: the aqueduct, which was bored first, and the railroad tunnel, which was bored afterwards using the first bore for access. Once the aqueduct tunnel was completed, drilling and blasting crews dug channels to the alignment of the railroad. This gave construction crews multiple faces, including the east and west portal, from which to bore the tunnel, that greatly speeded construction. The aqueduct was holed through in February 1927, with some of the final charges ceremoniously detonated by United States President Calvin Coolidge, remotely using a telegraph line from Washington, D.C. The railroad tunnel was completed by July of that year, and the first train passed through in February 1928. A public ceremony was held officially opening the tunnel on February 26th. As built, the Moffat Tunnel is 16 feet wide and 24 feet tall. According to author William D. Middleton, the tunnel is 32,799 feet long, just a little more than six miles. The east portal is an elevation of 9,198 feet above sea level; the grade westbound through the tunnel rises at 0.3 percent cresting near the middle of the tunnel at 9,249 feet, and then descends on a 0.9 percent grade to the west portal at an elevation of 9,085 feet. Building the tunnel lowered the D&SL's crossing of the Continental Divide by slightly more than 2,400 feet, and allowed the railroad to eliminate its most difficult operations, including all of the 4 percent climb and the tightest curves. While the Moffat Tunnel is high enough to receive significant snowfall, winter operations are much easier to cope with than over the Giant's Ladder.

With the completion of the Moffat Tunnel, the D&SL abandoned its old Rollins Pass crossing, but the whole railroad was still effectively a dead-end coal branch into the Rockies. Today, it may seem strange that with all the work of building the Moffat Tunnel, when it opened, trains could only travel as far west as Craig, Colorado—there was no immediate potential for through traffic.

This situation did not last long, however. The D&SL's visions of reaching Utah directly on their own line were finally abandoned in favor of a route from Bond, Colorado, through Gore Canyon to connect with the Rio Grande's mainline to Utah. The Rio Grande was at first opposed to this connection, known as the Dotstero Cutoff, but it eventually acquiesced. Construction began in November 1932, and was completed less than two years later in June 1934. This line was among the last transcontinental links built in the United States, and one of the very last bits of major new railway construction. It gave the D&SL the outlet to the west that it needed, fulfilling the spirit of David Moffat's ambition, if not the letter of his intent. The remainder of the D&SL line to Craig has survived as a coal branch ever since.

In 1947 the Denver & Salt Lake was merged into the Rio Grande. In the 1980s, the Rio Grande came under common management with the Southern Pacific and in 1996, the combined Southern Pacific-Rio Grande system was bought by the ever-expanding Union Pacific. Union Pacific was quick to close Rio Grande's Tennessee Pass crossing in favor of the Moffat route, thus leaving this line as one of the few remaining railways in the Colorado Rockies—an area once blanketed by railways. Today the Moffat line is very busy handling UP's freights, as well as those of Burlington Northern Santa Fe, which acquired trackage rights over the route as a condition of the UP's acquisition of SP and Rio Grande. You can ride through the Moffat Tunnel on Amtrak's daily *California Zephyr*, and in the winter on the *Rio Grande Ski Train*, which connects Denver and Winter Park.

The Moffat Tunnel hosted the famous *California Zephyr* between 1950 and 1970. The *Zephyr* was jointly operated by the Burlington, Rio Grande, and Western Pacific, and connected Chicago to Oakland, California. This view from a Budd Vista Dome was made as the *Zephyr* approached the east portal in April 1966. After the *California Zephyr* was discontinued, Rio Grande continued to run a pocket streamliner under the name *Rio Grande Zephyr* until 1983. Today Amtrak's *California Zephyr* uses the tunnel.

Richard Jay Solomon

Japanese Shinkansen

JR West's *Nozomi 500* was the fastest regularly scheduled train in the world when it entered service between Osaka and Hagata in March 1997. While its top running speed of 186 mph (300 km/h) is matched by other high-speed services, such as the French TGV *Atlantique*, the *Nozomi 500* earned its reputation because it had the fastest station-to-station running times.

Boarding a modern Shinkansen train at Toyko Central Station, you marvel at its sleek, streamlined profile. Settling into your seat, you gaze out of the window as the train glides out of the station, past the vast megalopolis that comprises greater Tokyo. At first, the train doesn't run significantly faster than any other modern electric train, but once beyond the dense urban sprawl, it gradually gathers speed. Nearby scenery zips by your window, yet the distant mountains to the west seem to just loll by at a relaxed pace. Every so often you blast through a tunnel, but the train is pressurized to avoid any serious discomfort. Rail traffic coming against you on the opposite iron races by frequently, presenting just a momentary "snap" at the window as the trains blur. It's only when you reach your destination and stand on the platform to watch an express train overtake the one you just got off, that you begin to appreciate the speed at which the Shinkansen trains travel. Bearing down on you at the rate of nearly one-half-mile every ten seconds, you don't see or hear a train coming until it's practically at your spot on the platform. Whooshh! It's gone so quickly your senses barely have time to comprehend the event. That's the beauty of the Shinkansen!

Birth of High-Speed Rail

The world's first true high-speed railway system was Japan's creative solution to its burgeoning transport problem. Japan is composed of four large islands. Although these have considerable landmass, most of the terrain is too rugged and mountainous for urban development and industry. Roughly 40 percent of the Japanese population re-

A mosaic at Tokyo Central Station marks the Shinkansen's "0km Point," the place from which all points on the New Tokaido Shinkansen are measured.

sides in a heavily industrialized area that represents only one percent of the country's landmass. This is a long and relatively narrow strip of land on the south and east coast of Honshu, Japan's largest island.

Japan enjoyed a period of vigorous growth following the destruction of World War II. By the mid 1950s, the Japanese railway network, (known by the roman letters JR), had reached capacity on its busiest route, the Tokaido Line, which connects Japan's two largest cities, Tokyo and Osaka. Expansion was limited by several severe capacity restraints. Japan's railway network was built to a smaller standard than most American and European railways—Japan's standard track gauge is just 3 feet 6 inches (1,067mm), much narrower than the Stephenson standard of 4 feet 8.5 inches.

The Tokaido line passed through the thickly populated urban landscape, hemmed in by buildings, which limited the railways ability to expand capacity. Another problem was level road-crossings, over a thousand, which slowed operations and made traffic expansion difficult. The Tokaido Line was engineered to an early standard, following a relatively circuitous route, meandering from city to city and station to station. JR boosted capacity by electrifying the route, but this gain was soon overshadowed by continued rapid traffic growth.

To overcome the capacity constraints on the Tokaido Line, JR decided to design and build an entirely new railway between Tokyo and Osaka. The new railway was meant to augment the existing network rather than replace it. In so doing, JR abandoned the standards set

by the rest of the network. New railway construction is traditionally designed to adhere to existing network parameters, since the advantages of integrated operations normally outweigh advantages achieved by using different engineering standards. But there were precedents for adopting non-conforming gauge parameters. In the late 1830s, Isambard Kingdom Brunel chose a broad track gauge (7 feet, 1/4 inch) for his Great Western Railway. Although this move generated great controversy at the time, Brunel felt that a broader gauge would allow him to run faster trains and provide greater capacity and comfort. While his argument had some merit and his broad gauge network eventually reached much of the southwest of England, the gauge incompatibility proved irksome and inconvenient to travelers and shippers. Ultimately the Great Western was re-gauged to permit compatibility with the rest of the standard gauge British network.

However, JR decided that the existing parameters of its narrow gauge railway network were inadequate for a newly designed high-speed line, so it followed the Brunelian approach, adopting a much broader standard for its new railway, the Shinkansen. Like Brunel, JR forsook compatibility for speed and capacity. Unlike Brunel, they chose 4 feet 8.5 inches, the international standard gauge, rather than a completely new width. Wider tracks not only allow for larger railway cars, but more importantly, provided the greater stability needed for high-speed operation.

In conjunction with the wider track gauge, is a wider loading gauge. Loading gauge determines the size of the railway cars. Other significant engineering changes were implemented as well. Instead of using 1,500 volt direct current electrification that was already employed on JR's meter gauge lines, the Shinkansen used a modern, high voltage alternating current electrification system, based on the successful use of a similar system in France. The first Shinkansen lines were electrified at 25kV at 60Hz.

The new railway and the new trains were designed simultaneously, allowing the two designs to achieve a maximum potential. So, many difficulties that often can occur with new train designs as a result of infrastructure incompatibility were avoided. Construction of the Shinkansen began in 1959. It progressed according to a very tight schedule in order to be fully operational in time for the 1964 Olympic Games held in Tokyo.

The New Tokaido line, as the first Shinkansen route is known, was engineered to very high standards. The entire line is grade separated with no level crossings with roads or other railways. Large sections of the line are elevated on viaducts and bridges, not just in cities, but over farmland and meadows. Tracks are laid with concrete ties and continuous welded rail, and the route has very gentle curves with long sections of tangent track. The New Tokaido Line follows a much straighter route than the older, narrow gauge Tokaido Line, shortening the run between Tokyo and Osaka by roughly 25 miles. Yet, the new line is hardly level, and in fact features fairly steep grades. On much of the route the maximum gradient is 2 percent—nearly as steep as many of the mountain grades in the western United States. Steep grades were made possible by designing the new trains with sufficiently powerful motors to sustain high speeds. Originally, the New Tokaido Shinkansen was a single route connecting two main terminals with just 10 intermediate stations, allowing for a very simple track arrangement that avoided complex junctions and interchanges.

In the 1960s the Shinkansen set new standards for high-speed rail service that were not matched or exceeded anywhere in the world for more than a decade. In the evening twilight, a Series-100 train zips through a station southwest of Tokyo.

The entire route uses directional double track with dispatcher-controlled passing sidings at stations. This arrangement maximizes the use of the double track route by allowing local trains to get off the mainline while loading passengers, and permitting express trains to pass without having to slow or stop.

Although the Shinkansen was a state-of-the-art modern electric railway with extremely high engineering, it did not employ revolutionary technology. Almost all the technology used on the line had been developed previously; all JR did was perfect existing systems. One of the most significant innovations on the line was its exclusive use of cab-signaling to control train movements. While various cab signal systems and automatic train control had been used for decades to augment lineside automatic block, and other conventional signaling, the Shinkansen is considered the first railway to rely exclusively on cab signals. Even today, nearly 40 years after the Shinkansen's public debut, many heavily traveled railways still rely on lineside signaling, although other new high-speed lines, such as those in France, follow the cab signaling precedent established by the New Tokaido line.

The Bullet Train

The Shinkansen high-speed trains also employed a highly refined design using established technology. Simplicity of operation was a key consideration in the design of the "Bullet trains." After years of intensive research, JR settled upon a streamlined electric multiple-unit design outfitted with high-powered electric motors, enabling the trains to both reach and maintain high speeds. A multiple-unit passenger consist doesn't use a locomotive; instead, each car has electric traction motors driving its axles. Initially, the Bullet trains were arranged in 12-unit, double-ended sets. One advantage of a multiple-unit design is that a high-powered train can maintain relatively low axle loading (the amount of weight placed on each axle). Another advantage is its double-ended design, ideally suited to the simple arrangement of the Shinkansen system's terminal facilities. The Bullet train has a Janus-like quality: both ends have a "face" and there is no "tail," an arrangement that negates the need for run-around tracks and locomotive turning facilities.

In the 1930s, the benefits of streamlining were definitively examined. By the early 1960s, when the Shinkansen's "Bullet Trains" were designed, there was little doubt that fast trains required a streamlined design. The characteristic appearance of their streamlining and exceptional speed quickly earned them the nickname "Bullet Trains," a moniker that stuck, and has been handed down and applied to later generations of Shinkansen high-speed trains, as well.

Above: JR's Series-0 high-speed trains were the original "Bullet Trains." Although very few of these 1960s-era designed trains remain in revenue service, they are still one of the most recognized high-speed trains in the world. Their streamlined treatment shares a resemblance to early passenger jet airplanes, which date from the same period.

Below: A Series-0 "Bullet Train" pulls out of the passing siding at Nishi-Akashi, Japan. Most stations have dispatcher controlled passing sidings that allow express trains to zip around local trains that have paused for a station stop.

A Spectacular Success

The New Tokaido Shinkansen debuted, as scheduled, in October 1964, and initially the 320-mile long line hosted 30 round trips a day. There were two types of service: *Kodama* trains that made most of the intermediate stops; and *Hikari* express runs that only stopped at the largest stations. Initially, both services used the characteristic Series-0 "Bullet trains" in 12-car configurations. While JR had at first planned for top speeds of 160 mph, the New Tokaido Shinkansen trains were limited to 130 mph. Despite the slower speed, the Shinkansen was still by far the fastest railway in the world when it opened, a distinction it held for decades to come. From the start, the Shinkansen's ridership soared and JR added many additional trains. By the late 1960s, there were 80 round trips per day. By the early 1970s, the trains were lengthened from 12 to 16 cars to increase capacity.

The New Tokaido Shinkansen's large, early ridership and the exposure it gained as a result of the 1964 Olympic Games put the railway in the world spotlight. Japan's state of the art, high-speed trains spurred interest in similar railway programs by many nations, including the United States. In the mid 1960s, the American federal government provided funding for high-speed railway research and development. This ultimately led to improvements on the heavily traveled North East Corridor between Boston, New York, and Washington D.C., which at the time was privately run by the Pennsylvania and New Haven Railroads. The first *Metroliners*, paid for by the federal government, were high-speed multiple units designed in the shadow of the Shinkansen Series-0, albeit without the Shinkansen' streamlining.

The success of the New Tokaido Shinkansen had a serious effect on Japan's transportation policy. Within a few years of the Shinkansen's debut, internal airline service between Tokyo and Osaka was scaled back, and additional Shinkansen routes were planned. In the early 1970s, work began on the New Sanyo Shinkansen, which was effectively an extension of the original Shinkansen route. This route, like the other new Shinkansen lines that followed, was engineered to even higher standards than the New Tokaido Line. Design improvements included heavier track structure, and even gentler curves in order to allow for faster speeds.

Later Shinkansen routes traversed more rugged terrain and required more substantial engineering than the original line. For example, the 344 mile (554 km) New Sanyo Line that connects Osaka with Hagata was built with roughly a third of its entire route in tunnels. Some of these tunnels are among the longest in the world, including the famous 11.6 mile (18.7 km) Shin-Kanmon Tunnel, which runs beneath the sea, connecting the Japanese islands of Honshu and Kyushu.

Progress on the Shinkansen network progressed more slowly than hoped, but over time, the Shinkansen system has been extended widely over Japan, and more routes are planned. There are two separate Shinkansen networks, and since the break-up and privatization of JR in 1987, there are three different companies that operate Shinkansen trains. The original Shinkansen network reaches south and west of Tokyo. The other network connects Tokyo with cities in the north and east of Japan. While both Shinkansen systems serve adjacent platforms at Tokyo Central Station, there are no through services, and the systems use different trains. There isn't even a track connection at Tokyo Central.

There are two important reasons for this network discontinuity, one technical, the other demographical. The two systems use different alternating current 25 kV electrification standards. The original network is electrified at 60Hz, while the later system that runs north and east, is electrified at 50Hz. This reflects the difference in the Japanese power grids north and south of Tokyo. The difference in frequency could be easily overcome with modern technology, as it is on the U.S. Northeast corridor. However, Tokyo is the primary destination for many Shinkansen passengers and since it is relatively easy to change trains at Tokyo Central, there is little incentive to provide through services.

More, Better, and Faster

The enormously high ridership and frequent service had nearly worn out the New Tokaido line in its first decade. By the mid 1970s, as the first extensions were underway, JR needed to replace the fleet of original Series-0 "Bullet trains." Replacement trains were built to the same specifications as the first and did not incorporate significant technological or stylistic changes. Later, in 1985, the Shinkansen Series 100 trains appeared; these featured a streamlined design with a more pointed nose than found on earlier Series-0 trains.

While the Series-0 may still reflect the popular image of what a "high-speed train" looks like, they are dinosaurs in comparison with the most recent designs. Since privatization, radically different Shinkansen trains have been developed. These new trains have a very different appearance, and can operate much faster than the original Series-0. Superior streamlining, combined with the development of modern three-phase alternating current traction systems (similar to that used on contemporary high horse-power diesel-electric locomotives in the United States such as Electro-Motive's SD70MAC and SD90MAC, and General Electric's AC4400CW), have permitted some Shinkansen trains to regularly oper-

A JR East Series-200 Shinkansen accelerates away from Tokyo with a full load of passengers. With the privatization of the JR network, JR East inherited the Northern Shinkansen routes among other lines including some very heavily used Tokyo suburban routes. Today JR East is one of the world's busiest passenger railways, carrying as many as six billion passengers a year.

ate at speeds up to 186 mph (300 km/h).

The fastest and most impressive of all the new Shinkansen trains is JR West's Series-500 that operates on the *Nozomi 500* super-express lines. The original *Nozomi* service began operation with new Series-300 trains in March 1992. Running at a top speed of 168 mph (270 km/h), the *Nozomi* express trains offered a significantly faster service on the New Tokaido Line than the traditional service. In 1993, *Nozomi* services were extended all the way to Hakata. The development of the Series-500 trains in the mid 1990s allowed JR to reclaim the status of the fastest, regularly scheduled trains in the world, a title that had been taken from it by the French TGV in the 1980s.

Series-500 trains are fantastic, modern machines with a super-streamlined futuristic appearance unlike anything else on steel wheels. The long, tapered nose and striking blue-and-gray livery make the Series-500 a symbol of speed and progress. Even regular Shinkansen passengers, accustomed to the sight of state-of-the-art trains blasting past at super-high speeds were amazed by the sight of these new trains. When the *Nozomi* blitzes a station at speed, hold your breath! One can savor just a momentary glimpse as the wind rushes past following the train's lightning-like run.

The first regularly scheduled *Nozomi 500* service debuted in March 1997 on JR West's Osaka to Hagata run. This run may have surprised some observers because initially the "World's Fastest Train" did not serve Toyko! By the end of the year, *Series-500* trains were operating to the Japanese capital. The Series 500 train reaches the same top limit 300 km/h (186 mph) imposed on regularly scheduled TGV services. The reason the *Nozomi 500* is considered the fastest is not just because of its top speed, which is matched by other services, but because

A detailed view of a Series-300 Shinkansen train at Tokyo Central Station depicts the train's modern streamlined treatment. Shinkansen trains' streamlining is designed to keep noise levels within legal limits as well as to lower wind resistance for high-speed operation.

of its fast time between stations. Like New York Central's *Twentieth Century Limited*, the *Nozomi 500* is an "extra fare" train. It is very special and expensively run, and a privilege afforded only by the railway riding elite. Other *Nozomi* services are handled by Series-300 and very modern Series-700 trains. Although also very impressive, these trains do not reach the highest speeds.

As the New Tokaido Shinkansen approaches its 40th year of operation, it is still the busiest high-speed railway in the world. Today, as many as 11 round trips per *hour* operate between Toyko and Osaka, and there are plans to boost service to 15 round trips per hour in the next few years.

Off the Beaten Track

Not all of the Shinkansen lines have been newly built. Some of the feeder routes on the northern Shinkansen routes were converted from existing narrow gauge lines to 4 feet, 8.5 inch gauge and equipped for Shinkansen trains. This is a compromise situation. The old lines retain sinuous alignments precluding the top speeds achieved on newly built Shinkansen lines, yet they allow for a faster through-train service to Tokyo than could be afforded by conventional trains. The Shinkansen trains that operate on these converted lines must conform to the constraints of a narrow loading gauge, and are noticeably smaller than the trains that strictly operate on the high-speed lines.

You don't need to visit Japan to see a JR "Bullet train." In 2001, one of the Series-0 cab cars was restored and sent to the British National Railway Museum at York for display. There it sits in the company of other famous fast trains, Sir Nigel Gresley's famous *Mallard*, and Robert Stephenson's pioneering *Rocket*.

Channel Tunnel

The *Eurostar* is the best-known railway service that uses the Channel Tunnel between England and France. Presently, all *Eurostar* trains use London's Waterloo International and must reach the station over traditional lines that do not permit super-fast running. A new high-speed line called the Channel Tunnel Rail Link is under construction; when completed, it will allow *Eurostar* to travel at top speeds and will serve a new international station at London St. Pancras. In July 2001, a *Eurostar* passes Wandsworth Road in London on its way to the Channel Tunnel.

Today, at Waterloo Station in London, you may board any of dozens of suburban trains traveling as near as Vauxhall (just one stop out), or to any number of more distant stations on the old Southern Railway in England. Adjacent to the suburban terminal is the modern looking Waterloo International, where you can catch the sleek, streamlined *Eurostar*—a modern high-speed train that will whisk you below the English Channel to France. You have a choice of services: In just three hours you will be in the French capital, Paris; or in two hours, forty minutes, you can travel to Brussels, Belgium via Lille, France. While taking the *Eurostar* is slightly more involved than boarding a local train for Clapham Junction, today Paris is just another railway destination from London.

The Channel Tunnel is perhaps the most significant railway infrastructure in Europe. It links Britain with the Continent and is one of the most heavily used railway routes in the world. Although it was completed in 1994, after almost seven years of construction, the Channel Tunnel was almost 200 years in the making.

With just 18 miles across the Straits of Dover between the shores of Britain and France, the vision of a tunnel was first seriously suggested in Napoleonic times. In 1800, a generation before the first public steam railway, French engineer Monsieur Mathieu proposed the first trans-channel tunnel. Over the generations, various plans for tunnels and bridges were drafted and discussed, some quite earnestly. Tunnel companies were formed and construction projects begun, but until modern times, all the schemes stalled in their formative stages and were abandoned. Many railway books mention the Channel Tunnel years before it was built. In 1935, an 8-page

article in *Railway Wonders of the World*, describes a host of different Channel Tunnel schemes. Yet it would take another six decades before trains actually rolled below the English Channel.

Impediments to the building and completion of the Channel Tunnel were more political and financial than technological. Long standing animosities between France and Britain needed to be set aside before the project could be undertaken, while the enormous cost of building the tunnel needed to be settled.

The tunnel consists of three separate bores. The two outside bores, 7.6 meters in diameter, each carry a single railway track; a smaller central bore is a service tunnel designed for maintenance and safety. Cross passages and air ducts connect the three tunnels at regular intervals to allow for the regulation of airflow in the tunnels, and provide a safe escape in the case of emergencies. Since the tunnel is 31.4 miles long (50.5 km), of which 24 miles are located up to 148 feet (45 meters) below the bottom of the Channel, safety is a primary concern. A variety of systems monitor conditions in the tunnel to assure the safe passage of trains. There are two crossovers, roughly one-third of the distance from the portals that allow trains to pass from one track to the other.

The service tunnel breakthrough was accomplished in December 1990. It was another three-and-a-half years before the rail tunnel was ready. In May 1994, it was officially opened by Britain's Queen Elizabeth II and French president Francois

A London-bound *Eurostar* has just exited the Channel Tunnel at Folkstone and races past the LeShuttle car and truck ferries terminal. Another *Eurostar* can be seen in the distance.

Mitterrand. A railway shuttle service for heavy over-the-road trucks began a few weeks later, followed by through all-rail freight services between Britain and the Continent, and finally, at the end of the year, high-speed *Eurostar* passenger trains began operations.

The tunnel is operated by Eurotunnel, which provides rail-ferry services for automobiles and trucks at regular intervals throughout the day. Large terminals are located near each portal to load autos and trucks on and off rail-ferries. The rail-ferry is marketed as the *Eurotunnel Shuttle* and employs specially designed railway cars and locomotives. Each *Eurotunnel Shuttle* train is powered by a pair of high-horsepower locomotives that use a B-B-B wheel arrangement and take power at 25 kV 50Hz. For both practicality and safety concerns, the rail-ferries operate in a push-pull arrangement; a locomotive is positioned at each end of the train. The auto-carrying ferries use sets of 12 cars that are 18 feet, 10 inches tall, and 85 feet, 10 inches long, which Eurotunnel advertises as the largest railway vehicles in public use in the world. Truck ferries use railcars that are taller, but not as long as the car ferries. All-rail freight trains travel directly from various points throughout Britain to Continental destinations, including terminals in Germany, Luxembourg, Italy, France, and Spain.

The *Eurostar* high-speed passenger consists are the best-known trains that pass through the Channel Tunnel. Although they feature distinctive exterior

styling, they are just a technological variant of the French Train à Grande Vitesse (TGV), designed in the late 1970s and early 1980s for high-speed services within France. On the specially built high-speed tracks in France, the *Eurostar* trains travel at a maximum speed of 186 mph (300 km/h), the same top speed as other modern TGV designs. In the tunnel top speed is only 100 mph, and presently *Eurostar* trains are limited to 100 mph or less on traditional railway lines in Britain. While France had completed its high-speed links to the Channel Tunnel in time for the 1994 opening, the high-speed lines on the British side of the tunnel, known collectively as the Channel Tunnel Rail Link (CTRL), are still under construction as of this writing in early 2002. They are expected to be completed in two stages, opening in 2003 and 2006, and will allow top speeds of 186 mph (300 km/h) between the tunnel and London, making them by far the fastest railway lines in Britain. Portions of the CTRL will run parallel to existing routes, but nearing London, it will utilize a series of new tunnels to reach the city center. With the completion of the CTRL the *Eurostar* will serve a new international terminal at a fully renovated and modernized St. Pancras Station (see pages 68 to 71).

While the Channel Tunnel is presently the longest railway tunnel in Europe, it is not the longest railway tunnel in the world. Japan's Seikan Tunnel that connects the main Honshu Island with the sparsely populated northern Hokkaido Island is the world's longest undersea tunnel. It was completed in March 1988, and at 33.5 miles (54 km) long is slightly longer than the Channel Tunnel. It was originally intended for the standard-gauge high-speed Japanese Shinkansen (see pages 150 to 156), but only regular, meter-gauge trains serve it today on a daily, but infrequent schedule.

Bibliography

Books

All Stations: A Journey Through 150 years of Railway History. New York: 1978 (no author listed).

Albi, Charles, and Kenton Forrest. *The Moffat Tunnel, A Brief History.* Golden, CO: (Colorado Railroad Museum), 1984.

Allen, G. Freeman. *The Fastest Trains in the World.* London: Scribners, 1978.

Bell, J. Snowdon. *The Early Motive Power of the Baltimore and Ohio Railroad.* New York: Angus Sinclair Co., 1912.

Biddle, Gordon. *Great Railway Stations of Britain.* London: David and Charles, 1986.

Binney, Marcus, and David Pearce, eds. *Railway Architecture.* London: Bloomsbury Books, 1979.

Bruce, Alfred W. *The Steam Locomotive in America.* New York: Bonanza Books, 1952.

Burgess, George H., and Miles C. Kennedy, *Centennial History of the Pennsylvania Railroad.* Philadelphia: Pennsylvania Railroad Company, 1949.

Bush, Donald J. *The Streamlined Decade.* New York: George Braziller, 1975.

Byron, Carl R. *A Pinprick of Light, The Troy and Greenfield Railroad and Its Hoosac Tunnel.* Shelburne, VT: (New England Press), 1995.

Casey, Robert J. and W.A.S. Douglas. *The Lackawanna Story.* New York: McGraw-Hill, 1951.

Churella, Albert, J. *From Steam to Diesel.* Princeton, NJ: (Princeton University Press), 1998.

Condit, Carl. *Port of New York, Vols. 1 & 2.* Chicago: Univ. of Chicago Press, 1980, 1981.

Conrad, J. David. The Steam Locomotive Directory of North America. *Vols. I & II.* Polo, IL: Transportation Trails, 1988.

Conrad, Ernst. *Bernina Express.* München, Germany: 1986.

Cupper, Dan. *Horseshoe Heritage, The Story of a Great Railroad Landmark.* Halifax, PA: Horseshoe Curve National Historic Landmark, 1996.

Diehl, Lorraine B. *The Late Great Pennsylvania Station.* New York: Houghton Mifflin Co., 1985.

Droege, John A. *Passenger Terminals and Trains.* New York,: McGraw-Hill, 1916.

Drury, George H. *The Historical Guide to North American Railroads.* Waukesha, WI: Kalmbach, 1985, 1993.

——. *Guide to North American Steam Locomotives.* Waukesha, WI: Kalmbach Publishing Co., 1993.

——. *Santa Fe in the Mountains.* Waukesha, WI.: Kalmbach Publishing Co., 1995.

Dubin, Arthur D. *Some Classic Trains.* Milwaukee: Kalmbach Publishing Co., 1964.

——. *More Classic Trains.* Milwaukee: Kalmbach Publishing Co., 1974.

Evans, Martin. *Pacific Steam, The British Pacific Locomotive.* Hemel Hempstead, Herts, United Kingdom: Model Aeronautical Press, 1961.

Farrington, Jr., S. Kip. *Railroads at War.* New York: Coward-McCann, Inc., 1944.

——. *Railroading from the Rear End.* New York: Coward-McCann, 1946.

——. *Railroads of Today.* New York: Coward-McCann, 1949

Fischler, Stan. *Next Stop Grand Central.* Ontario: Boston Mills Press, 1986.

Garmany, John B. *Southern Pacific Dieselization.* Edmonds, WA: (Pacific Fast Mail), 1985.

General Motors. *Electro-Motive Division Operating Manual No. 2300.* La Grange, IL: (General Motors), 1945.

Harlow, Alvin F. *Steelways of New England.* New York: Creative Age Press, 1946.

——. *The Road of the Century.* New York: Creative Age Press, 1947.

Harris, Ken, ed. *World Electric Locomotives.* London: Ny Jane's, 1981.

Haut, F.J.G. *The Pictorial History of Electric Locomotives.* Cranbury, NJ: Barnes, 1970.

Hofsommer, Don. L. *Southern Pacific 1901-1985.* College Station, TX: Texas A&M, 1986.

Hollingsworth, Brian. *Modern Trains.* London: Arco, 1985.

Hollingsworth, Brian, and Arthur Cook. *Modern Locomotives.* London: Crescent Books, 1983.

Hungerford, Edward. *Men of Erie.* New York: Random House, 1946.

Jackson, Alan A. *London's Termini.* Newton Abbot: 1969.

Kiefer, P.W. *A Practical Evaluation of Railroad Motive Power.* New York: 1948.

Kirkland, John, F. *Dawn of the Diesel Age.* Pasadena, CA: Interurban Press, 1994.

Klein, Maury. *Union Pacific, Vols. I & II.* New York: Doubleday and Company, Inc., 1989.

Karr, Ronald Dale. *The Rail Lines of Southern New England.* Pepperell, MA: Branch Line Press, 1995.

Kratville, William, and Harold E. Ranks. *Motive Power of the Union Pacific.* Omaha, NE: Barnhart Press, 1958.

Lamb, W. Kaye. *History of the Canadian Pacific Railway.* New York: Macmillan Co., 1977.

Marre, Louis A., and Jerry A. Pinkepank. *The Contemporary Diesel Spotter's Guide.* Milwaukee: Kalmbach Publications, 1985.

Marre, Louis, A. *Diesel Locomotives: The First 50 Years.* Waukesha, WI: Kalmbach Publications, 1995.

Marshall, John. *The Guinness Book of Rail Facts and Feats.* Enfield, Middlesex, United Kingdom: Guinness Superlatives, 1975.

Meeks, Carroll L. V. *The Railroad Station.* New Haven, CT: Yale Univ. Press, 1956.

Middleton, William D. *When the Steam Railroads Electrified.* Milwaukee, WI: Kalmbach Publications, 1974.

——. *Grand Central . . . the World's Greatest Railway Terminal.* San Marino, CA: Golden West Books, 1977.

Middleton, William D. *Manhattan Gateway: New York's Pennsylvania Station.* Waukesha, WI: Kalmbach Publications, 1996.

———. *Landmarks on the Iron Road.* Bloomington, Indiana: Indiana Univ. Press, 1999.

Morgan, David P. *Steam's Finest Hour.* Milwaukee, WI: Kalmbach Publications, 1959.

Mullay, A. J. *Streamlined Steam, Britain's 1930s Luxury Expresses.* NewtonAbbot, Devon, United Kingdom: 1994.

Mulhearn, Daniel J., and John R. Taibi. *General Motors' F-Units.* New York: 1982.

Nock, O.S. *LNER Steam.* London: 1969.

———. *British Locomotives of the 20th Century, Volumes. 2 & 3.* London: 1984.

Overton, Richard C. *Burlington Route.* New York: Alfred A. Knopf, 1965.

Potter, Janet Greenstein. *Great American Railroad Stations.* New York: Preservation Press, 1996.

Protheroe, Ernest. *The Railways of the World.* London: George Routledge & Sons, no date (1920?).

Ransome-Wallis, P. *World Railway Locomotives.* New York: Hawthorn, 1959.

Reck, Franklin M. *On Time: The History of the Electro-Motive Division of General Motors.* Dearborn, MI: General Motors, 1948.

———. *The Dilworth Story.* New York: McGraw Hill Book Co., 1954.

Roth, Leland M. *Understanding Architecture: Its Elements, History and Meaning.* Westview Press, 1993.

Semmens, P.W.B. *High Speed in Japan.* Sheffield, United Kingdom: 1997.

Signor, John R. *Southern Pacific-Santa Fe Tehachapi.* San Marino, CA: Golden West Books, 1983.

Simmons, Jack. *Rail 150, The Stockton & Darlington Railway and What Followed.* London: Eyre Methuen, 1975.

Sinclair, Angus. *Development of the Locomotive Engine.* New York: MIT Press, 1970.

Snell, J. B. *Early Railways.* London: Octopus Books, 1972.

Solomon, Brian. *The American Steam Locomotive.* Osceola, WI: MBI Publishing, 1998.

———. *Bullet Trains.* Osceola, WI: MBI Publishing, 2001.

———. *Railroad Stations.* New York: Metro Books, 1998

———. *Trains of the Old West.* New York: Michael Friedman Publishing Group, 1998.

Solomon, Brian, and Mike Schafer. *New York Central Railroad.* Osceola, WI: MBI Publishing, 1999.

Staufer, Alvin F. *Pennsy Power III.* Medina, Ohio, 1993.

———. *Steam Power of the New York Central System, Volume 1.* Medina, Ohio, 1961

Staufer, Alvin F., and Edward L. May. *New York Central's Later Power.* Medina, Ohio: author, 1981

Steinman, David B., and Sara Ruth Watson. *Bridges and Their Builders.* New York, 1957.

Stilgoe, John R. *Metropolitan Corridor.* New Haven, CT: Yale Univ. Press, 1983.

Stretton, Clement E. *The Development of the Locomotive.* London: Bracken Books, 1989.

Swengel, Frank M. *The American Steam Locomotive: Volume 1, Evolution.* Davenport, IA: Midwest Rail, 1967.

Taber, Thomas Townsend, and Thomas Taber Townsend III. *The Delaware, Lackawanna & Western Railroad, Part One.* Muncy, PA: Thomas T. Taber III, 1980.

Talbot, F. A. *Railway Wonders of the World, Volumes 1 & 2.* London: Cassell & Co., 1914.

Taylor, Arthur. *Hi-Tech Trains.* London: Apple Press, 1992.

Westing, Frederic. *Penn Station: Its Tunnels and Side Rodders.* Seattle, WA: Superior Publishing, 1977.

White, John H., Jr. *Early American Locomotives.* New York: Dover, 1979.

Whitelegg, John, and Staffan Hultén. *High Speed Trains: Fast Tracks to the Future.* Burtersett, Hawes, North Yorkshire, UK: Leading Edge Press and Publishing, 1993.

Winchester, Clarence. *Railway Wonders of the World, Volumes 1 & 2.* London: 1935.

Young, William S. *Starrucca the Bridge of Stone. Published privately, 2000.*

Zimmermann, Karl R. *Erie Lackawanna East.* New York: Quadrant Press, 1975.

———. *The Remarkable GG1.* New York: Quadrant Press, 1977.

Periodicals

Baldwin Locomotives. Philadelphia, Pa. [no longer published]

Diesel Era. Halifax, Pa.

Jane's World Railways. London.

Journal of the Irish Railway Record Society, Dublin, Ireland.

Locomotive & Railway Preservation. Waukesha, Wis. [no longer published]

Modern Railways. Surrey, United Kingdom.

Rail. Peterborough, United Kingdom.

RailNews. Waukesha, Wis. [no longer published]

Railroad History, formerly *Railway and Locomotive Historical Society Bulletin.* Boston, Mass.

Railway Age. Chicago and New York.

Railway Gazette. 1870-1908, New York.

Official Guide to the Railways. New York

Today's Railways. Sheffield, United Kingdom.

Thomas Cook, European Timetable. Peterborough, United Kingdom.

Trains. Waukesha, Wis.

Vintage Rails. Waukesha, Wis. [no longer published]

Index